Irwin Bazelon

Irwin Bazelon. (Photograph courtesy of Patricia Layman Bazelon)

Irwin Bazelon

A Bio-Bibliography

David Harold Cox

Bio-Bibliographies in Music, Number 80
Donald L. Hixon, *Series Adviser*

GREENWOOD PRESS
Westport, Connecticut • London

Library of Congress Cataloging-in-Publication Data

Cox, David Harold.
　　Irwin Bazelon : a bio-bibliography / David Harold Cox.
　　　p.　cm.—(Bio-bibliographies in music, ISSN 0742–6968 ;
　no. 80)
　　Includes bibliographical references (p.　), discography (p.　),
　and index.
　　　ISBN 0–313–30550–1 (alk. paper)
　　　1. Bazelon, Irwin—Bibliography.　2. Bazelon, Irwin—Discography.
　I. Title.　II. Series.
　ML134.B29C69　2000
　780′.92—dc21　　　00–030901

British Library Cataloguing in Publication Data is available.

Library of Congress Catalog Card Number: 00–030901
ISBN: 0–313–30550–1
ISSN: 0742–6968

First published in 2000

Greenwood Press, 88 Post Road West, Westport, CT 06881
An imprint of Greenwood Publishing Group, Inc.
www.greenwood.com

Printed in the United States of America

The paper used in this book complies with the
Permanent Paper Standard issued by the National
Information Standards Organization (Z39.48–1984).

10　9　8　7　6　5　4　3　2　1

Dedicated to the memory of

Irwin Bazelon

(1922-1995)

Contents

Preface

As with other volumes in the series Bio-Bibliographies in Music, the objective of this book is to record details of the source material pertaining to Irwin Bazelon and his works, as a guide for those wishing to undertake further research into the composer and his music. Since Bazelon's life as a professional composer was rich and varied and touched on many different individuals and situations, it is inevitable that no list of sources could be comprehensive, but it is hoped that most, if not all, of the most important sources of information about the composer have been included.

The volume is arranged in the following manner:

(1) A short biography of Irwin Bazelon. It includes a description of his character and personality, which was as original and as striking as his music, a brief account of his life, which followed an unorthodox path for a twentieth-century composer in that he supported himself and his art-music by various freelance compositional activities rather than by teaching in a university, and an assessment of his significance as a composer.

(2) A selection of Bazelon's unpublished writings on music. These are included to preserve primary sources for posterity and because they reveal many of the issues that concerned the composer during his creative life. They comprise an early statement of Bazelon's creative aesthetic in the form of an unpublished letter to the editor of The New York Times, explaining how the composer found inspiration in the frenetic pace of city life, mirrored in microcosm at the racetrack; a selection of aphorisms which Bazelon was in the habit of jotting down; and other material which only survives as sketches. The selection ends with three longer excerpts: the first, an example of the "angry" Bazelon, from an article discussing the position of the serious composer in American society; the second, of a more technical nature, taken from a lecture

on writing for percussion given at a composition workshop; and the third, a general introduction to his music, one of a number of lectures, usually entitled "The Invisible Composer," which he gave in various forms in the final years of his life. The collection shows Bazelon to have been a man of strong views, often forcefully expressed, and while it is possible that he might have been more circumspect in print, the material reveals many of the beliefs and attitudes of the composer.

(3) A list of works, in chronological order of composition. Bazelon frequently used subtitles and these are given on a second line in bold type except for those works whose initial title is a musical genre and subtitle a description of its instrumentation. The list includes a description of the instrumentation of each orchestral work and the names of those to whom works were dedicated and/or by whom they were commissioned. It includes information on publication and details of the first performance, where known, giving the date, location and names of the performers. The location of the original manuscript is also given. Each manuscript is in the composer's hand except where stated. In many cases, the published scores are reproductions of the composer's manuscript and, as Bazelon usually composed directly into the final score, few, if any, sketches survive.

This is the first attempt to list all Bazelon's works in chronological order. I have therefore devised a numbering system which will, I hope, stand the test of time. Many incomplete lists of Bazelon's works can be found in dictionaries and in the catalogues of music publishers. A number of catalogues of Bazelon's works were produced by his various publishers and agents including:

Boosey and Hawkes	1967, 1971
Novello	1982, 1986
E. Snapp Inc.	1992
Theodore Presser	1996

Although the dates of composition in these sources were provided by Bazelon, a number of inaccuracies and contradictions can be found.

The primary source that has been used for dating Bazelon's works is the information given by the composer at the end of the score. This normally comprises a date of completion, together with, in the mature works, the place in which the composition was written. In most cases Bazelon just indicated the month in which the work was finished, but he did sometimes specify an exact date and occasionally only the year of completion. If the date of composition is not given at the end of the score but is known from other evidence then the date is given in brackets followed by an explanation of its origin. There are also a few examples of two dates being used to indicate the period over which the work was composed.

It is evident from the number of examples that can be found that when Bazelon revised (or renamed) a work, he altered the year of composition at the end of the score, but not the month. The month in which a work was revised is therefore doubtful but is still given in the list as it appears at the end of the score.

Much of Bazelon's early music was reproduced and bound by various local companies that offered such services. These scores are not, of course, available from these companies, even if they still exist. A few early works published by Peer-Southern and by Weintraub Music Company are still available. Bazelon's music was published by Boosey and Hawkes from 1963-1978 and by Novello from 1978-1990. The published works that were not specifically retained by these companies are now available from Theodore Presser.

(4) A list of other works. As a professional freelance composer, Bazelon supported himself by writing music for a variety of commercial assignments. These works are listed separately from his art-music. The arrangement is alphabetical and the list is divided into six categories: arrangements, commercials, films (documentaries and industrials), incidental music for theatrical productions, library music for Boosey and Hawkes written under the pseudonym Budd Graham, and television and movies.

Bazelon's commercial output was extensive, covering a period from the mid-1950s to the mid-1970s. Dates of composition are given where they are known. Many of the manuscript scores are undated. Some works only survive as recordings. The location of each manuscript is given, if it still exists. All the manuscripts are in the composer's hand.

The assignments that Bazelon undertook often enabled him to experiment creatively with new ideas. As a result there are a number of instances in which music of commercial origin subsequently formed the basis, in whole or in part, of serious art-music and these are cross-referenced.

(5) A list of Bazelon's published writings. This includes the two editions of his book on film music, *Knowing the Score: Notes on Film Music,* some early review articles and a number of letters.

(6) A bibliography of articles and reviews arranged alphabetically by author. The list also includes a number of dictionary entries on the composer and the references to programme notes that are listed in *The Music Index,* the subject-author guide to music periodical literature. The most important source for the list was the material that Bazelon kept in his personal papers and it therefore includes all the references that he thought were significant. Amongst the omissions from the list were some early references whose sources were too imprecise to trace, references where the content was too inconsequential to be of any value, and sources that were duplicated by syndication. As many of the sources are of an ephemeral nature, an indication of their contents has been included, particularly where they contain useful biographical information or significant comments by the composer. Quotations from the text, of a length permitted by the laws of copyright, have been used when appropriate. It has also been possible to give an indication of the wide range of opinions that were offered in response to Bazelon's music through the quotation of comments

selected from press reviews. The extensive use of literal quotation has been avoided and researchers are encouraged to discover the full content of these sources for themselves.

(7) A discography of Bazelon's recorded works. All formats (LP, cassette, CD) are included. The list is arranged alphabetically by work. Each entry includes: (1) the recording company, number, date and format, (2) the names of the performers and (3) details of the other works issued on the recording. A separate list includes a group of works recorded by Boosey and Hawkes and written under the pseudonym of Budd Graham.

(8) A description of the relevant contents of three archive collections including the Bazelon Collection at the Library of Congress, and the Leon Stein Collection at DePaul University.

(9) An index of references in the bibliographic sources: to art-music, to other works listed by commercials, documentaries, films and television, incidental music and the NBC-TV news theme, to reviews of recordings and of *Knowing the Score: Notes on Film Music,* and to bibliographic references indexed in chronological order by year.

(10) An index of references to persons, places, musical events and organisations.

I acknowledge the generous assistance given by a number of people and organisations: Edward G. Bazelon, Jacqueline Bazelon, David T. Bazelon, Robert Beaser, Richard Rodney Bennett, David Bernstein, Tom Broido (Theodore Presser), Donald Casey (Dean of Performing Arts, DePaul University), Chris Cleeren (B.R.T.N.), Roslyn Cox, Carmel Daly, James V.D'Arc (Brigham Young University Film Archives), Susan Dienelt, Gene Deitch, Don DeLillo, Scott Dunn, Giles Easterbrook (Novello), Frank Epstein, Harold Farberman, Lukas Foss, Michael Gross, David Hancock, Carter Harman (C.R.I.), Jonathan Haas, Addie Herder, Don Hixon and the staff at Greenwood Press, Kaylie Jones, Julian Koenig, Dorothy Lawson, Alan Mandel, Maria Matthiessen, Wanda Maximilien, William Moersch, Fred Papert, Liza Redfield, Timothy Reynish (Royal Northern College of Music), Leonard Rosenman, Alice Ross, Judith Shatin, William Smart (Virginia Center for the Creative Arts), Elizabeth Snapp, Vivienne Spratt, Leon Stein, Katharine Washburn, Stefan Weisman (Boosey and Hawkes), Richard Wellish, Roger Ziegler, staff at the following: Birmingham Public Library, Library of Congress, Library of Performing Arts, Lincoln Center, New York, New York Public Library, Library of Trinity College Dublin, University College Cork Boole Library, Library of University College Dublin, University of Birmingham Music Library, University of Sheffield Music Library.

Most of all, however, I acknowledge the total commitment, energy and enthusiasm given to me in the preparation of this book by Cecile Gray Bazelon. She allowed me free access to her husband's personal files, her collection of his press articles and reviews and his manuscripts, tapes and recordings. She provided me with much information that I would not otherwise have been able to obtain and she helped me to avoid a number of significant factual errors. Without her unstinting help, patient support and thoughtful advice, this book would not have been possible.

Biography

The qualities of integrity and vision, characteristics of the true artist, are perfectly exemplified by Irwin Bazelon. He devoted his life to the art of composition. He followed his vocation without any support from one of the most common sources of artistic patronage in the twentieth century, a post in a university. He was, instead, one of the first composers to use extensive freelance commercial activities to support the composition of art-music. He did not compromise his artistic integrity in either genre. The two aspects of his creative personality are strongly linked; his music is not academic, in the sense of being erudite for its own sake, and, although his musical language is unique, elements of rhythmic vitality and a remarkable sense of instrumental colour give it immediate appeal. His artistic vision was inspired by his experience of the energetic pace of city life, specifically Chicago and New York. This is expressed through a highly developed rhythmic language, a language that he could demonstrate vocally, and is evident in his music through the unmistakable Bazelon pulsation of a series of unpredictable accents and syncopations that creates a powerful and aurally challenging rhythmic drive.

The many facets of Bazelon's complex character are reflected in the wide emotional range of his music. He was a man of enormous energy. The novelist Don DeLillo described an evening spent in the company of the composer (and his wife) as exposure to a human crossfire of ideas and opinions. A witty raconteur, he could be dynamic and forceful and he enjoyed making an unforgettable initial impact upon individuals and social occasions. There is a strong similarity between the comments he would make to someone he was meeting for the first time and the bold aggressive openings of many of his works. He could also be gentle, tender and solicitous and those qualities are reflected in the slower, quieter sections of his music, passages that could also be dark, brooding and pulsating with restrained energy. The contrast between a forceful, dynamic exuberance and an intense, powerful introspection is evident in his music. The result is music that is both disturbing and challenging. One might not imagine the personality that produced it until, after meeting the composer, it became obvious that its deep intensity and breadth of expression was a perfect reflection of his inner life.

Irwin Allen Bazelon was born on June 4, 1922 in Evanston, Illinois. He was the elder of two sons born to Roy and Jeanette Bazelon. Although he used the name Irwin professionally, he was often jokingly depreciative of it. From the age of four, on the recommendation of his uncle, Judge David L. Bazelon, he was known as Bud to his family and friends. On the birth certificate his father is described as a travelling salesman. In fact, Roy Bazelon was involved in many different business enterprises before he finally took up a long, venturesome career in real estate in Florida. Bazelon's grandparents were Russian Jews who came to America from Russia in the 1890s. Little is now known of the family history before that generation. The family might have originated in Southern Europe since the unusual surname Bazelon could be a corruption of the word Barcelona. Such Mediterranean origins could also account for Bazelon's striking appearance, handsome with steel-grey hair and piercing blue eyes.

Like many large immigrant families starting a new life in the New World, the Bazelons embraced an American tradition that was both dynamic and competitive. Brought up during the difficult years of the Depression, Bazelon was keenly aware of the opportunities provided by American commercial enterprise. While he chose the more challenging route to success of the artistic life and often remarked that he felt excluded by what he described as the "greatest super-business culture the world has ever seen,"[1] there is, paradoxically, within his musical language, the energy and dynamism of a quintessentially American composer.

In his early, formative years the duality later evident in his work was already apparent. The young Bazelon was artistic, musical and creative. He was also a gifted athlete and, for a time, his father hoped that his son would have a career as a baseball player. Although disappointed in this dream and mystified by the uncompromising originality of his musical language, Bazelon's parents supported his aims and objectives, with some occasional reservations when the artistic path became difficult. Bazelon acknowledged his debt to them on a score of his *Short Symphony* (1961) which he presented to them on its publication in 1967, with the inscription:

To Mother and Dad who worried with me through many moments of anxiety, offered sympathy and a helping hand when it was most appreciated and perhaps least understood - from their son and the first member of the family to take up this extremely painstaking way of life as a composer of serious music - gratefully and with love.

A bout of scarlet fever in his childhood left Bazelon with a perforated eardrum and severe hearing loss in one ear. This affliction increased a tendency to introspection and was only cured by an operation performed by an ear surgeon when he was an adult. His partial deafness increased his sensitivity to sound as he struggled to make aural sense of his environment, including developing the ability to read lips. Once the problem was solved he was left with an extremely acute ear, able to execute his creative imagination without recourse to the piano as a compositional tool. In his mature years he did not make extensive revisions to his work. The cure also had the effect of liberating his artistic imagination as "the violent, silent world" inside him "erupted."[2] The music could be as volatile as the man.

Among Bazelon's early musical experiences were piano lessons from his cousin Irving Harris, composing popular songs and playing in a jazz band. Although he left the world of popular music behind, the influence of jazz remained with him all his life, even if distilled to a rhythmic essence. His work was often described as making unusual use of jazz idioms. These influences helped the composer sustain sections impelled by rhythmic drive and are also reflected in the scoring of works such as *Symphony No. 3* (1962) and *Churchill Downs* (1971). An uncompromising style such as Bazelon's needs an element to which the listener can relate, and the composer's unorthodox use of jazz idioms creates a link with a vernacular musical language.

The course of Bazelon's life was dramatically changed by the experience, at the age of 17, of hearing a performance of Beethoven's Seventh Symphony by the Chicago Symphony Orchestra. He decided he would become a composer, one working in a symphonic tradition exploiting the resources of orchestral sound. In 1942 he transferred from his liberal arts course at Northwestern University to study music at DePaul University. He was fortunate to study composition with Leon Stein, a kind and sympathetic teacher, who responded positively to Bazelon's thirst for knowledge which outstripped the restraints imposed by the curriculum. A number of works survive from this period. Although juvenilia, they are interesting in that they show a rapid acquisition of compositional skills and the dawning of an artistic vision. The earliest, *Fugue for Piano,* dates from March 1942. Another, *Humouresque* (1944) was Bazelon's first publicly performed work when a version for two pianos was played at DePaul. The performers included his first formal piano teacher, Magdalen Massmann.

After graduating from DePaul with a Bachelor of Music degree in 1944 and a Master of Music degree in 1945, Bazelon went to Yale to study with Paul Hindemith but found the "Prussian taskmaster's"[3] teaching methods unsuited to his still developing creative talents. In 1946 Bazelon found a more understanding teacher in Darius Milhaud at Mills College, Oakland, California. Milhaud was the most important, direct formative influence upon his creative life. The close relationship that developed between the two is most evident in Bazelon's *Chamber Symphonette No. 1* (1947) which is distinctively French in its manipulation of musical material and sonority. In California he also took the opportunity to study Advanced Analysis with Ernest Bloch.

Bazelon's first significant achievement was to win second prize in a competition organised by the National Federation of Music Clubs with his *String Quartet No. 2* (1946). The quartet is one of a group of works in which the youthful composer flexes his compositional muscles and allows his creative imagination full flow. These works also include the three *Piano Sonatas* (1947, 1952, 1952), the second *Sonata for Violin and Piano* (1949), a powerful and tautly-structured work, and the remarkable *Concerto-Symphonique* (1948) for piano and orchestra, a dramatic and forceful piano concerto, half an hour in length. In a letter to Leon Stein written on December 9, 1947, Bazelon stated that he wanted it to be "a mature musical utterance, not a poor example of a floundering youth."[4] Of all the early works it most anticipates the power and originality of the mature Bazelon, dramatically projecting a solo instrument against a large opposing ensemble in a way that the composer later favoured.

The far-sighted creative imagination and the mastery of large-scale resources of the *Concerto-Symphonique* reveals a composer fully aware of the achievements of Bartok, Stravinsky, Milhaud and Varèse, but already capable of imposing his own personality on the traditions he inherited. Bazelon took an awareness of the power of rhythmic drive from Bartok and Stravinsky and sensitivity to orchestral sonority from Milhaud, complemented by a realisation of the expressive power of the percussion section of the orchestra from Varèse. Like many composers who develop an original musical language, Bazelon initially had an eclectic personality, drawing on a wide range of sources, including serial technique and jazz, but with the vision to be able to synthesise them into his own personal expressive voice.

After completing his studies with Milhaud in 1948, Bazelon came to New York. It was an ideal place for a young composer to be, exposing him to a ferment of ideas and creative originality. He met performers such as Bernardo Segall, who gave the première of his *Piano Sonata No. 1,* and his wife the dancer Valerie Bettis, for whom Bazelon wrote the ballet suite *Three Abstractions* (1948). He met other young composers, writers and painters at the Edward MacDowell Colony where he spent several summers in residence with the aid of colony fellowships.

Whilst studying in California Bazelon had supported himself by working as a railroad reservations clerk. He found a similar job in New York. It lasted for seven years until he realised that "I couldn't do it another day or else I'd be a reservations clerk the rest of my life."[5] Fortunately Bazelon was able to earn a living from composition. In 1953 he began to write music for commercials, for products as diverse as Ipana toothpaste, Buitoni pasta and Noxzema skin-cream. As his reputation grew, more assignments followed. He wrote the incidental music for two productions by John Houseman for the American Shakespeare Festival Theater, *The Taming of the Shrew* (1957) and *The Merry Wives of Windsor* (1959), music for various film documentaries, including the art films *The Ivory Knife* (1965), a film without narration about the painter Paul Jenkins and *New York 100* (1967) about the painter John Hultberg, music for TV productions including Budd Schulberg's *What Makes Sammy Run?* (1959) (in which he also appeared playing the piano), and Bud Greenspan's *The Glory of Their Times* (1969) and *Wilma* (1977). The most lucrative of all these activities, in terms of return for creative effort, was the 8-second theme heard for many years at the close of the NBC Public Service News Broadcasts (1963).

Bazelon made no musical compromises in his commercial work. He did not write "jingles". He wrote in a modern idiom, describing himself as "the father of contemporary music in commercials."[6] His activities as a freelance composer enabled him to experiment creatively. He discovered how to make large sounds with limited resources and unexpected sonorities by using instrumental spacing in unique ways. There are a number of examples of cross-fertilisation between his commercial work and his serious art-music. The great creative effort required to fulfil a large number of commercial assignments produced a composer with a remarkable sensitivity to sound and an inventive imagination. Bazelon was always interested in new combinations of sonority. He wrote a number of works such as *Sound Dreams* (1977) in which the musical argument is textural rather than thematic.

In the 1950s composers rarely divided their creative efforts between commercial activities and serious music. Bazelon had established a reputation in both fields. In 1961, with his career at a crossroads, Bazelon and his wife (he had just married for the fourth time), the artist Cecile Gray, went to Hollywood. What seemed a natural move to develop his reputation as a composer of film music, was, in retrospect, a mistake. Bazelon's music was too original for the tastes of Hollywood producers still firmly rooted in the lush sounds of late nineteenth-century romanticism. After nine months, the Bazelons came home. The experience did, however, have the effect of focusing Bazelon's mind on his creative objectives. The evolution of a mature, distinctively original style can be dated from his return to New York and the realisation that he should fulfil his own artistic vision. This new creative direction is shown by the start of a substantial symphonic output.

The experience of life in the cities of Chicago (the city of his birth) and of New York (the city of his choice) was the aesthetic catalyst for the development of a radically new musical language. Bazelon rejected the impression given by the wide open spaces of the west in favour of a different, but equally valid, American vision, one inspired by the pace of city life. He later remarked that "the rebellious mutterings, cross-rhythms and nervous tension and energy of the city"[7] could be found in his music. He stated that "the alterations of mood, color and dramatic flair are a direct expression of the constant changes of pace, the rhythmic beat of life in the big metropolis."[8] He also found a microcosm of city life at the racetrack, where each horse race captured a wide range of human emotions: "hope, anxiety, joy and disappointment."[9]

The first powerful expression of this aesthetic occurred in the *Short Symphony* (1961), subtitled *Testament to a Big City*. It was also his first real breakthrough as a composer of national significance. In 1959 Bazelon used a windfall from racetrack winnings to record *Concert Ballet: Centauri 17* (1959). On a trip to Washington he met Howard Mitchell, the conductor of the National Symphony Orchestra. He played him the recording and showed him the score of the symphony. Bazelon had expected that he would only have a few minutes with the maestro and it was an hour before he mentioned that his wife was waiting outside in the car. The symphony was programmed for performance in 1962 with the composer conducting. The concert attracted considerable advance publicity because of its many different unusual and interesting aspects: a composer who played the horses rather than the piano, a composer inspired by his experience of the frenetic pace of city life and a composer struggling to survive in a materialistic culture. The music lived up to expectations and favourable press reviews led to Bazelon's music being published by Boosey and Hawkes.

More performances of Bazelon's orchestral works followed. Hans Schweiger conducted the Kansas City Philharmonic in the world premiere of *Symphony No. 1* in 1963. In an associated event, Bazelon took part with Schweiger and the composer Roger Sessions in a discussion panel organised by the Music Critics Association. In 1966 the Seattle Symphony Orchestra under Milton Katims gave the world premiere of *Dramatic Movement for Orchestra* (1965), the first movement of *Symphony No. 4*. The preparation of this work was subsequently featured in a TV documentary on the orchestra.

While most conductors now have unlisted phone numbers, it was possible in the 1960s for composers to call conductors personally. One day, going through Indianapolis en route to a concert, Bazelon decided to ring Izler Solomon. He looked in the phone book, found the number and called him. Solomon invited him over. When they met the two men were struck by their close physical resemblance. Solomon agreed to conduct the world premiere of *Symphony No. 5* (1967) and later recorded the work with the Indianapolis Symphony Orchestra.

The genesis of the Sixth Symphony illustrates the interaction between Bazelon's various composing activities. In 1967 he met the director Jules Dassin who asked him to write the music for his documentary about Israel during the Six-Day War, *Survival 67*. He was a natural choice because of the dramatic style of his music and his friendship with the scriptwriter, author Irwin Shaw. When in 1968 Bazelon was commissioned to write a work to celebrate the 100th anniversary of the founding of the Temple B'nai Jehudah in Kansas City, the symphony naturally developed out of the musical material of the film. Bazelon also decided that the first performance of the sixth symphony should be given under an amended title: *Symphony No. Six "Day-War."*

Although much of Bazelon's output in the 1960s and 1970s was written for orchestra, he also wrote a number of important works for smaller ensembles. His most significant pieces include the *Brass Quintet* (1965), a genre he called "the string quartet of the twentieth century,"[10] and *Churchill Downs* (1971), for fourteen players, inspired by his first experience at the Kentucky Derby, expressed through a remarkably original rhythmic language in which jazz influences are apparent.

The primary force of Bazelon's music is often rhythmic. He rarely described his methods of composition but he did sometimes comment that he would invent the rhythmic sequence of passages of music first and consider the pitched material later. A few purely rhythmic sketches survive to support his use of this method. The powerful rhythmic drive is created by unpredictable syncopation, off-beat accents, irregular groupings and unexpected triplets (he often said, in jest, that the triplet was his heartbeat), broken up by the dramatic use of silence, sometimes likened to the rhythmic essence of jazz without the underlying beat.

In the music Bazelon wrote up to *Phenomena* (1972), he frequently indicated rapid tempo changes (slow to fast or the reverse) within the bar. After that work these changes, which are difficult for a large ensemble to achieve in performance, are indicated by the use of sloping beams, a device Bazelon learned about from his friend Richard Rodney Bennett. Both these methods of trying to capture graduated tempo change are part of what Bazelon described as a lifelong attempt "to find the cracks between the notes."[11] The result of this search for rhythmic freedom is the pulsating excitement of long stretches of fast ostinato-driven music or the brooding, even melancholic, uncertainty of slower passages. The impact on the audience was unsettling, because the music lacked any regular pulse. Bazelon realised that his music was challenging, noting defiantly that audiences "may not like it but they won't be bored by it."[12]

Bazelon's second success in a composition competition came in 1970 when he won the Cleveland Orchestra's Blossom Music Center's competition for a fanfare. In a little over a minute the *Dramatic Fanfare* displays the Bazelon dynamic energy in microcosm. It is still played to call audiences to their seats in the orchestra's summer home.

In 1974 Bazelon spent a period as composer-in-residence at Wolf Trap, Virginia. Much of that year, however, was spent in a painful reappraisal of his position as a creative artist that eventually led to a decision to give up his commercial activities. His farewell to this side of his creative life is symbolised by two works written in that year; his book, *Knowing the Score: Notes on Film Music,* in which the aesthetics of such activities are ruthlessly examined and one of his finest works, *Propulsions*, written for a large percussion ensemble, in which 113 percussion instruments are played by seven performers. Many of the new sonorities with which Bazelon experimented as a freelance composer involved percussion and his interest in exploiting the expressive potential of these instruments resulted in this work. As a demonstration of the expressive possibilities of the medium, it attracted the interest of many percussionists and led to a remarkable series of works which combine pitched and percussive sonorities including *Double Crossings* (1976), *Concatenations* (1976), *Triple Play* (1977), *Cross-Currents* (1978) and *Partnership* (1980).

The year 1975 was more profitable for Bazelon. His book *Knowing the Score* was published. *Propulsions, Woodwind Quintet* (1975) and *A Quiet Piece ... for a violent time* (1975) were given their world premieres. Bazelon was awarded a Musicians Fellowship Grant by the National Endowment for the Arts. Even more lucrative, although he did have to lay out a $2 stake, was a famous win of $4828 at Aqueduct racetrack in May. Brass Bell, Carl Swaps, Twin Angle and the numbers 10-6-1 brought the composer a lasting reputation as a racing tipster.

After the death of author James Jones in 1977, Bazelon wrote *Sound Dreams* in memory of his friend. The score is typical of the more reflective music Bazelon composed in his later years. The title page quotes a phrase by James Jones: "You composers live in a world of Sound Dreams."

In 1981 and 1983 Bazelon was a composing fellow at the Virginia Center for the Creative Arts. He later persuaded his father to endow the Jeanette Bazelon Composer's Studio there in memory of his mother. Bazelon always enjoyed colony life (he and his wife had spent a memorable summer at Yaddo in 1969) and he realised the value of contact with creative artists from different disciplines. Many of his friends were artists and writers. He was a cultured man with interests ranging from literature and the visual arts to aspects of science such as astronomy. An avid reader of poetry, his tastes were evident in the choice of modern poets like Wallace Stevens and Hart Crane whose works he set to music.

In 1983 Bazelon was awarded the prestigious Koussevitsky Prize for his contribution to contemporary music, a prize which led to the composition of *Fusions* (1983). The prize symbolised his emergence as a major American composer with a growing international reputation, with performances of *De-Tonations* (1978) by the Orchestre Philharmonique de Lille in 1981 and *Propulsions* and *Churchill Downs* at the Royal Northern College of Music, Manchester, England in 1982.

At the same time Bazelon's natural abilities as a communicator made him much in demand as a public speaker. He took part in the Symposium on Technology and the Humanities in the Conference on World Affairs at the University of Colorado at Boulder in 1981. He was on a panel including Virgil Thomson and Willard Van Dyke discussing "Music for Documentaries" at the American Film Festival in the same year. He was involved in a number of workshops on composition organised by ASCAP. In 1984 he joined Morton Gould, Elie Siegmeister and John Harbinson in a panel discussion, "Trends in Contemporary Orchestral Music," at the 38th National Conference of the American Orchestra League in Chicago. He gave a lecture on music in contemporary culture titled "The Concert Composer - An Invisible Artist" to universities and music schools across America. Although he had never held an academic post, apart from teaching a course on film music at the School of Visual Arts in New York from 1968 to 1972, he was able to establish an instant rapport with music students. They responded to his direct and forceful approach and to the rebellious streak in his nature.

Bazelon returned to symphonic composition in the 1980s with Symphonies no. 7 (1980), no. 8 (1986), no. 8½ (1988) and finally no. 9 (1992). The unusually named *Symphony No. 8½* was so called because Bazelon already had a vision of his final ninth symphony, the setting of Hart Crane's long poem *The Bridge* (1930) which he left unfinished at his death. In fact the symphony dedicated to Sunday Silence became his ninth and *The Bridge* would have been his tenth. The period also produces an extensive exploration of the concerto repertory, with works for trumpet *Spires* (1981), for clarinet *Tides* (1982), for piano *Trajectories* (1985), for trombone *Motivations* (1986) and for cello *Entre Nous* (1992). Bazelon's music was taken up by a new generation of talented young performers and this led to the composition of works including *Imprints* (1978) for Rebecca LaBreque, *Suite for Marimba* (1983) for William Moersch, *Trajectories* for Wanda Maximilien, *Alliances* (1989) and *Entre Nous* for Dorothy Lawson.

Bazelon's work had long had the enthusiastic support of Frank Epstein (New England Conservatory) who commissioned *Concatenations* (1976) and *Bazz Ma Tazz* (1993) and Timothy Reynish (Royal Northern College of Music, Manchester) who commissioned *Midnight Music* (1990). The premiere of this latter work and its subsequent issue on CD was combined with music by Richard Rodney Bennett for whom *Re-Percussions* (1982) was written and to whom *Symphony No. 8* was dedicated. Bazelon's music was also taken up by the conductor Harold Farberman and the two men worked so closely together on producing recordings of Bazelon's orchestral works that the composer came to refer to him affectionately as "my conductor."[13] The many favourable reviews that the recordings of Bazelon's music received testify to the sensitivity and insight that Harold Farberman brought to the performance and interpretation of difficult and challenging scores.

The most passionate advocate of Bazelon's music was his wife, Cecile Gray Bazelon. An artist herself, she understood the compulsion to create that drove Bazelon, supporting him and his work, once describing his music as "a study in organised hysteria."[14] He paid his tribute to her when he stated that "whatever I've become as a composer, I owe to my wife."[15]

A devoted member of the Bazelon household was a Yorkshire Terrier named Mr. Clem, purchased on the couple's honeymoon in Paris in 1960. One of the most striking sights of Bazelon's Manhattan neighbourhood was the composer striding along the sidewalk, composing and conducting his music, with the little dog running behind him, scurrying on his little legs to keep up. When Mr. Clem died after seventeen years, a lhaso-schnauzer named Miss Clementine eventually took his place but Bazelon was so upset by the loss of Mr. Clem that he never walked a dog again.

In 1990 the Bazelons bought a second home in Sagaponack, a small town on the south shore of Long Island. Bazelon worked there during the summer months, composing in a studio overlooking the garden.

Bazelon's last works show no diminution of his creative powers. In a final, extended farewell to a long creative life, however, many of his these works make use of material from his earlier, often unperformed pieces. This use of pre-existing material creates structural coherence by exploiting the formal integrity of the precursor. It often involves the rhythmic intensification of the original material. The correspondences that can be found include links between the *Concert Ballet: Centauri 17* (1959), *Excursion* (1965) and the first and third movements of *Midnight Music* (1990), between *Symphony No. 6* (1969) and *Re-Percussions* (1982), between *Phenomena* (1972) and *Memories of a Winter Childhood* (1981), between *Junctures* (1979) and *Fire and Smoke* (1994), between *Motivations* (1986) and *Bazz Ma Tazz* (1993), and most remarkably of all, in a link that spans the entire mature creative output, between the main theme of the third movement of the *Sonatina* (1952), the finale of *Symphony No. 4* (1964-1965), *Triple Play* (1977), *Symphony No. 7* (1980) and *Bazz Ma Tazz* (1993). Similar techniques were used to convert *Sunday Silence* (1990) into *Symphony No. 9* (1992) which Bazelon proudly described as the first symphony to be inspired by and named after a racehorse.

The final period also shows a new interest in writing for the voice with two works written for Joan Heller, *Legends and Love Letters* (1987) and *Four ... Parts of a World* (1991) and the unfinished *The Bridge*. They demonstrate sensitivity to the setting of the text that might seem surprising for a composer whose output had been almost exclusively instrumental. His sketches for *The Bridge* show that the composer gave long and careful consideration to the meaning of the text and how it should be declaimed by the voice.

The widespread recognition given to Bazelon's music in the last years of his life did not, however, include a performance by the Chicago Symphony Orchestra, the orchestra of the city of his birth. This was much to the frustration of the composer, especially given the role the orchestra had played in his youthful conversion to art-music. He did, however, receive a degree of recognition in his hometown when in 1984 the Chicago Civic Orchestra performed the *Short Symphony* and in 1992 the Chicago String Ensemble commissioned a work for string orchestra, *Prelude to Hart Crane's The Bridge* (1991). This was intended to be the opening movement of *The Bridge* and the only section of the work Bazelon completed.

Bazelon wrote music that was controversial. It is both challenging to listen to and difficult to play. This led to problems in obtaining further performances after the first, particularly in the final years of the century when the great increase in the number of American composers meant that there was so much more music available. Bazelon was a composer of honesty and integrity. He did not compromise; he chose to write serious art-music in a society increasingly swamped by the entertainment values of a mass culture. He spoke with a unique voice and he captured a personal vision with great intensity and dramatic impact. It is a vision, moreover, that may yet prove to be of great cultural significance as a powerful expression of the essence of human life - its turmoil, its contrasts, its frenzy, its moments of calm and tranquillity - in the great cities of the latter part of the twentieth century.

Bazelon died on August 2, 1995, from complications after heart surgery. He is buried in the Evergreen Cemetery, close to his Sagaponack home. A recording of the last movement of the *Symphony No. 5* was played at his funeral, at the wish of the composer. In a final gesture of defiance, the hearse caught fire on the way to the cemetery. Not surprisingly for a composer with a dramatic and instinctive sense of timing, the incident took place on the expressway at the exit to the racetrack.

Notes:

1.   Ziegler, Roger. "Last Interview: Composer for 21st Century." *The Southampton Press* (August 17, 1995).

2.   "The Ballad of Big Bud." *Time Magazine* (May 20, 1966).

3.   ibid.

4.   Leon Stein Collection, DePaul University.

5.   Rice, Pat. "Artists in Profile." *Creative Arts* (September 27, 1981).

6.   op.cit. note ii.

7.   Sleeve note ORS 78291.

8.   Sleeve note CRI SD 287.

9.   White, Jean. "Highly Touted Composer Nears the Home Stretch." *The Washington Post* (December 2, 1962).

10.   Cox, David Harold. "A World of Violent Silence." *The Musical Times* (October 1982).

11.   Letter from Scott Dunn to Cecile Bazelon, 1995.

12.   Barela, Margaret. "World premiere in Williamstown." *The Berkshire Eagle* (April 25, 1985).

13.   Sleeve Note AT 282.

14.   Rosenberg, Donald. "Music famous but not composer Bazelon." *Akron Beacon Journal* (November 6, 1979).

15.   Lane, Barbara Kaplan. "An Urbanite Composing in Rural Sagaponack." *The New York Times* (January 30, 1994).

Unpublished Writings

Letter to the New York Times dated October 30, 1962.

This letter was one of the sources Brookes Atkinson used in his column "Idolators of New York raise Cain." See Bibliography 93.

As a composer, I take exception to the fact that the American intellectual is repelled by the city. Because I deal in the world of sound, I find the city not a human wilderness, but an exciting human jungle: a jungle belching forth a cascade of brassy discords, rebellious mutterings, cross rhythms and the frenetic jostling of its inhabitants.

There has been a myth perpetrated in America that our music is only a national expression when it embodies the heritage of the frontier - of prairie and mountain - of the panoramic sweep of the "golden west." The fact is that today's "grass-roots" composer is a product of the urbanization of American life. The super-industrialized business culture of the Twentieth Century has given the big city composer an amplified voice and created a contemporary spokesman for the age.

If the city is barbaric and cannibalistic, I find this native savagery a source of creative galvanization. Without the city and its magnetic vitality, I would not have found my "own sounds" and developed my personal style of composition.

In my second symphony, *Testimonial to a Big City,* which I am conducting in its world premiere, December 4th in Washington, D.C., with the National Symphony Orchestra, I pay homage to my life in the city. Though this work is in no way programmatic (it is not a portrait or an attempt to describe the city), the heartbeat of Megalopolis is inherent in every bar of music.

Coincidentally, I find the pace of life in the city and the pulse of life at the racetrack commensurate. The racetrack has become a highly significant stream of action in adjunct to urban living. Operating on the periphery of the city, it is a capsule image of New York's emotional temperament. Here, all the forces of city life - anxiety, nervous tension, promise, in addition to elements of frustration, ambition and the quick response - function as an integral part of the scene. This image reflects itself through the mirror of my artistic imagination and finds its way to the written score. In fact, I recommend to any student of composition if he doesn't have an outside income to sustain himself as an artist in this culture, that he learn how to handicap racehorses. In time of emergency, this supplementary big city avocation can be a Godsend and one is not surprised at the number of composers to be seen at weekends at the local track. With money won at Aqueduct I recorded a concert ballet using members of the New York Philharmonic, a recording which abetted me in obtaining a performance of *Testimonial.*

Even the evil forces of the city, the triggered mechanisms of hate, anger and blind brutality operate in a positive way for they function as a constant thorn in the side of artistic complacency and make the artist aware of both his aesthetic and social responsibilities.

Bazelon habitually used to jot down remarks in the form of aphorisms. Some of these comments may have come from non-attributed sources while others were clearly of his invention. They give an interesting insight into the mind of the composer and the pithy style of expression that he favoured.

"Music: My Contract with Life." Reflections on Music and Art.

Music is not a profession: it is an incurable malaise. One is inoculated when young and impressionable and never recovers.

I am seldom deeply interested in young men of music. Show me twenty years of dedication and commitment, and I will take you seriously.

The wish to be a composer or writer or painter is sometimes greater than the "need" to compose, write or paint. Bogus emotions give birth to vulgar aspirations.

For many young pop-rockers, music is only a stepping stone to the ultimate aim of their life ... to become a film actor and celebrity.

A composer is a person who hears his dreams and thinks with his ears.

A composer, like an athlete, must stay in constant training, or his ears will become rusty.

Too much "serious music" makes a point of being "serious."

The great thing about popular music is that it doesn't stay popular too long.

Anyone who does what he/she wants to do, cannot be a failure.

A man's true enemies are often the members of his immediate family.

The general public is far more interested in how an artist earns his living, than they are in his work.

Writing music that is safe, non-controversial and pleasant sounding is like eating candy for breakfast, cookies for lunch and cake for dinner. You may not die from the diet, but the lack of variety leads to hardening of the aural arteries.

A celebrity is quite often someone who has done very little; and the whole world knows about it.

Some of the most imperious, power-hungry, success-driven persons I have known are not businessmen, lawyers, politicians or corporate executives: they are artists.

Being "into" music is not the same as music being "into" you ... one is an emotional involvement, a fascination with music; the other a way of life.

I love the art of music: it's only the life that's killing me.

I'm not afraid of death's final stroke. It's the raising of the axe that petrifies me.

Untitled and Undated Manuscript.

The musical dream can be a creative ensnarement - where the artist becomes a prisoner of his talent.

The never-ending disappointment of the composer saps his enthusiasm - sometimes leaving him bitter and disillusioned, terminating in an actual detestation of music. The constant reiteration of the problems surrounding the musical life can become a form of enervating dialogue that leaves him a victim of creative constipation.

Early reputations can fade, the musical society that made you famous can drop you like a hot potato. History is full of well-known composers who suffered the fate of over-exposure and of others whose reputations blossomed after they passed from the scene.

The musical dreams of many (based on achieving fame and fortune) can disintegrate into a kind of professional limbo - where the promise of their youth lingers on only as a faint memory - a dying song.

Notes and Reflections: (undated typescript).

When I was a young man, I thought the world was waiting for my next piece. It was a shock to discover it wasn't. YOU are waiting for your next piece, and its birth depends on whether you HAVE to write it. After 40 years, my enthusiasm is high; the urgency tempered. In time the next piece will be written;

it is ineluctable. Meanwhile, the unconcerned world will have to wait ... a little longer.

I stood on the bridge and scanned the parallel tracks until they converged into one through my squinted-eye. A locomotive appeared in the distance, a faint toy, recalling my childhood electric train. I remember sitting in the dark and watching my train brilliantly aglow with its lights circling the room. It was a fantasy vehicle, a magic carpet to dream of far-away places and things to come. As the engine grew closer and increased in size, it passed right under me, the engineer waving his cap and I returning his salute by raising my arm ... an exchanging signal that said hello and goodbye to a lost boyhood. (Is it any wonder that years later I worked for the railroad?). How I loved that little train ... the green engine and the shiny observation car with the name "Pleasant View" printed on the side ... It was a place in time when tomorrow was a word I did not understand. Has it been that long?

Walking through my boyhood playground, I was struck by its constricted enclosure. Years ago the fence seemed far away. Now it was less than a stone's throw. Nothing had changed: the neighborhood remained drab and timeless; the houses frozen in concrete. Even the candy store occupied its cellar premises across the street from the old man's tailor shop. If you updated the vintage car and returned the trolley, 50 years would pass untouched, undisturbed. Outside the gate to the corner, I turned north ... a remembered way back to another home. I started to run ... faster than ever before, only stopping to jump into my car and race to the airport.

Interview Idea: (undated manuscript).

Most people compose "songs." This country has been brainwashed by Tin Pan Alley.
1. My music - "a study in organised hysteria."
2. I don't live off "commissions." I commission myself.
3. No gimmicks: musicians do not "whistle harmonics" or "speak" through mouthpieces.
4. Music has no intellectual "hocus-pocus" or heroic philosophy. The merging of science, physics and art is not my reason for composing, or "my bag."
5. The musician of tomorrow will have to know as much about oscillators and filters as he does about sharps and flats. [He will be] part physicist, sound engineer, mathematical genius and musician.
6. Is the orchestra moribund? Is the audience moribund? The volume of noise has increased as the general ratio to talent has decreased.
7. More people are getting into music from non-musical origins than ever before.
8. Everybody writes "tunes," everybody composes. The unending money-rhythm and the electric guitar - a perfect match.

A Question of Talent (unpublished typescript, dating from the late 1960s). Many of the opinions were developed in *Knowing the Score: Notes on Film Music*.

The compelling fact about musical talent is that it is not a rarity. A great many people share the endowment. The elements of musical aptitude: a keen ear, rhythmic response and innate perception and sensitivity tap more than the proverbial few on the shoulder. And yet, given this parity of birthright, it is surprising how few are invested with that extra dimension, that ineffable life spark, the supreme dedication it takes to spend years developing a talent to the ultimate achievement of first-rate artistry. One can be born, or display early in life, all the accoutrements of talent and still not be blessed with the extraordinary measure of creative drive, energy and unquenchable love of music - the basic necessities that separate the artist from the would-be artist.

When it comes to evidence of musical talent, I am convinced after spending years dedicated to a musical life, that one cogent fact remains irrefutable: in America most people have come to believe that music talent is the ability to write a popular song, play a popular song and sing a popular song. How this came about is another story: suffice to say, that America's gigantic "Pop music propaganda machine" ... commonly referred to as the Show Biz Culture ... and the monopoly on the Mass Media enjoyed by the purveyors of prefabricated art and bogus culture, have substantially abetted in the wide-spread acceptance of this gross misrepresentation. The question of talent has nothing to do with whether or not pop music (the 1920 variety, the 1940 assortment or the 1970 package) is good, bad, right or wrong; what is germane is the understanding that the criteria for musical talent has been greatly influenced in the minds of most laymen, by the constant, never-ending visual and aural bombardment they receive at the hands of the Pop music industry. Just as the early movies usually depicted the image of the composer creating his masterpieces while seated at the piano coveting inspiration (a totally false conception of how the composer actually works), today's avid guitar-hungry addicts continue to perpetuate the myth that musical talent is synonymous with the writing, singing and playing of popular love ballads (old or new), politically inspired music-poetry and socially documented protest outpourings. Not the works themselves, that is a matter of aesthetic judgement, but the corporeal presence of their creators, performing from coast to coast (via TV, radio and film) and projecting their image to millions of impressionable people of how music is written and what constitutes genuine creative talent. If their musical gifts are to be taken as gospel, it would seem that talent is decidedly not uncommon or a rarity, but rather that it is ubiquitous. If you dilute the standards of excellence to include everybody, you end up by excluding nobody. It is a sad fact of life in our culture that more people are composing, writing and painting than ever before in history. I am not at all certain that our age represents an increase in ability in these directions over previous generations. With so many people making love to guitars, cradling the instrument love-child in their arms, pressing it to their bosoms and caressing its heart-strings, it hardly seems to matter whether honest feelings of musical expression are produced, or merely the glossy surface sounds invoked are enough. The wandering, roving minstrels of yesteryear have become the raving, rampaging wondering troubadours of today. In the matter of who has talent, the gift itself is negligible. The making of music is now a universal outlet for most young people and a part of their growing-up life cycle pangs. It is not to be confused with music as a way of life.

The historically accepted measuring rod for talent has been repudiated; in fact, the lack of a natural calling for music is not reason enough to take a back seat in its creation. As a result of this ambiguity surrounding the nature of musical ability, the culture seems to be manufacturing (on an assembly-line schedule) an entirely new breed of instant composers. Like instant coffee, quick lunches and fast-acting drugs, today's youth finds its own musical highs and lows without having to wait a lifetime for things to happen. The exhibited ability to write a song, coin a poetic phrase and strum a few chords has given rise to a distinct triple-threat status ... "Composer, Author and Performer" ... and this official knighthood has been bestowed on so many (usually by their own hand), that one wonders what the title actually designates anymore. They have dubbed themselves at twenty what past generations hoped to be at forty. The fever of activity belies the fact that the whirlwind creative storm is actually a dustbowl, kicking up a lot of sand, amplifying the hoopla and beating the drums of hollow chests. The noise is deafening. Everybody playing, singing and making an orgiastic display of musical togetherness. What all of this has to do with genuine musical talent and depth of artistic perception is a moot point. If the young need this form of strenuous musical gyration (God knows, I remember the Jitterbug era), that's perfectly all right but to confuse the madcap beehive of musical production with the art of music is foolhardy. A work of art is something greater than stimulated agitation, just as the art of composition is a bit more than writing a tune. The talented young musician of unusual sensitivity is aware that musical art attempts to go beyond the initial stimulus produced by a pleasant, singable melody, a graceful poetic line, a raucous rhythmic beat or a frenzied kinetic release: it attempts to interest the mind in a more pronounced abrasion than mere titillation ... hoping to engage it beyond the initial impact.

Notes for Composition Workshop. Writing Techniques for Percussion. Excerpts from a lecture given to the Peabody Composers Forum, Baltimore, Maryland, 1984.

For me, there is no orchestration. When I compose, the selection of instruments in their proper dramatic or lyric context is predetermined in my own mind as I am writing. The process of composition-orchestration is a simultaneous one without division.

I deal in what I refer to as rhythmic propulsion. While it incorporates some of the elements of Carter's Metric Modulation, it is not exactly the same thing. Quite simply it is the use of all time values (large to small), with metronomic limitations, interfused among each other to create variety and invention, adding up to a progressive explosion thrust forward, without the contours of constant movement flowing in one voice or another of the omnipresent 8th or 16th note. In this context, I have learned never to underestimate the value of a rest or a triplet.

Percussion and brass are such a vital part of my musical thinking because I feel they represent the string quartet of the 20th century. They bear the same relationship to our time as the string quartet did to the previous two centuries. Percussion and brass make-up the sound of today.

For me percussion instruments are not noise-makers. They are soloists, capable of extreme nuance, technical skill, rhythmic imagination and unlimited color dialogue. I've been accused of being a "closet percussionist," actually I'm a "re-percussionist." I've also had the happy fortune or misfortune as the case may be, of knowing many percussion performers, and I have learned from them how to write effectively for their instruments.

The Great Masters seldom used percussion (excepting mad Berlioz) for anything more than mere noisemakers of orchestral climax reinforcement. But in the last two decades or so, the percussionist has become a very potent weapon in the musical arsenal available to the contemporary composer.

As a young music student, I learned the art of cultivating an "eye" for pizzicato in cello and bass. This is relevant to percussion. Too much can destroy delicate balances, mask or bury musical ideas or even camouflage a lack of them. Too little is to miss the opportunity of adding just the right amount of musical spice needed to make a phrase or passage a successful realization. In the process I have recognized a basic truth: it is always the initial entrance of a new percussion sound that makes the greatest impact, especially the snare drum. Continued use has a tendency to pall, unless judiciously handled. Interestingly, I have never in all my pieces clashed cymbals. I suppose this represents to me the quintessence of the numerous 19th century orchestral scores I have heard in my lifetime. I've hit them, choked them, poked them, stroked them, nudged them, touched them with my fingers, nails and bass bow, but never have I clashed them face to face.

One of the most vital elements in composition, and often overlooked or even ignored by composers, is contrast. It is contrast that sustains interest and it goes hand-in-hand with instrumental color and dynamic pitch-shading (loud to soft, high to low). One must be careful in writing for solo percussion ensemble that you "do not shoot your bolt" too fast, otherwise you will have nothing left. It is controlled bombardment (especially with numerous players), invention and contrast that ensures the best realization of the power in the many instruments on hand, and eventually leading and highlighting any given climax.

Just as different mutes in brass instruments add color and nuance, a careful selection of individual mallets and sticks offer the composer a wide variety of contrast and shading to the varied instruments employed. I personally am fond of striking a high woodblock with a hard xylophone mallet in one hand, followed by an attack on a low timbale or tom-tom with a snare drum stick in the other hand. This may be closely shadowed by a series of drum rhythms using very hard (small) timpani mallets; three different color interpolations within a short framework of sound and time.

In my music, the varying relationships between relative pitches (high-medium-low), dynamics (loud, soft, slow to fast, fast to slow), often written in spatial notation, trigger a series of emotional explosions that propel the music forward. I try and interrelate the sounds of membrane, wood, steel, glass ... and silence. This includes techniques that involve gentle strokes, sharp blows, and friction, and, when desired, coaxing sounds that evoke gossamer webs of sound color, or, in some cases, increasing tension. I am a dramatic composer so that when I want a sharp accent, for example, I am inclined not merely to have a rim-shot but to add temple blocks, hit two bongos simultaneously and throw in for good measure, an anvil on a piece of railroad track. My theory is simple: if you are going to give the audience a jolt, make it a good one.

"The Concert Composer: An Invisible Artist." Lecture to Queen's College, October 15th, 1990.

Before I play my musical notes, I'd like to talk briefly about notes without music. Dylan Thomas said "a person is only an artist for a short time in his/her life; the rest of the time one is a human being" and, I might add, with other interests and distractions. Through the years, I have been a keen observer of the Pop Culture and the music it produces, even if its heartbeat runs directly counter clockwise to my own. I have concluded that America is a song-writing happy country. More attention and prestige is paid to these musician types in the mirror of public recognition and visibility than all the members of the fine arts combined. In fact, most people think a composer is a songwriter and that a musician plays in a rock-band. Well, what else would they think? Who else do they see? As a result, anyone contemplating a career as a "serious" (I really hate that word) concert composer must be acutely aware of the limited audience he is writing for, and of his place in this society. To disregard this awareness or confrontation, if you prefer, is to seal up one's eyes, ears and mind.

I was born in Chicago and became fascinated by music at an early age. During my high school years, I wrote pop songs and played piano in various pick-up local dance bands. And then one day it happened: an event that changed my life. One evening I wandered into Orchestral Hall and heard the Chicago Symphony. After the concert it suddenly struck me like a lightning bolt that one man, Beethoven, had written all the notes played by 100 musicians, and he did so without an arranger. And it dawned on me that the art of musical composition was the ability to invent, organize and develop musical ideas; to have the know-how to put a piece together, and it was a bit more involved than writing tunes or in today's vernacular, merging "funky" sounds. This revelation started my musical odyssey; to find my own sounds and hope, eventually, in the process to become a real composer. I entered DePaul University and after graduating, I studied briefly with Paul Hindemith at Yale. Following this hectic experience, I travelled to the west coast and became one of Darius Milhaud's first composition students at Mills College (after the Brubeck brothers), staying with him for over two years. I arrived in New York in 1948. At that time there were probably only about 300 concert composers in the United States. Today, ASCAP estimates 30,000. The joke going round asks: "What do you hit if you drop a brick from the Empire State Building?" The answer: a composer, naturally. With so many "emerging" composers making their appearance, I'm worried about what is to become of us "submerging" ones.

Today, the term "composer" is used rather loosely and does not mean what it once signified. Many do not read or write music and fall into the category of "Children of the Synthesiser." It seems to me that there are more non-composers writing music in one haphazard way or another than there are non-composers not writing music. And this phenomenon carries over into literature where there are 60,000 non-books published each year.

What does it mean to be a composer of concert music in 1990, the last decade of the 20th century, in the midst of the greatest super-business society ever placed on earth? A society that has spawned this elephantine pop music press communications culture, inculcating millions of impressionable adolescents with the incredible idea that show biz, entertainment, song hits, guitars, celebrity-hood and culture are synonymous terms. They are not. One truth I recognise: being a concert composer in this culture is not exactly a measuring standard for sanity. To me, the whole idea that the entire range and gamut of human emotions, sensitivities and nuances can only be expressed through a relentless rock-beat or ubiquitous pop-song borders on absurdity. To paraphrase Churchill: "Never before in history have so many had the opportunity to say so little, so often, with such overpowering network amplification."

In listening to the radio one discovers that the few classical music stations still operating (about 40 full time classical outlets out of some 8,000 commercial broadcasting wavelengths) offer a sea of tranquillity amidst the pounding surf of pop rock. Granted that music means different things to different people, and questions of "what is music?" and "what is art?" are being drastically revised these days, the fact remains that the concert composer occupies a marginal place in society. Our isolation and alienation is a monument to indifference. We are seldom seen; we have become invisible artists, infrequently heard and rarely is our work publicised. I'm reminded of Morton

Gould's great line: "If people like your music it's popular; if they don't like your music it's serious."

In today's musical world where more than 95% of the concert composers teach in colleges and universities, I am somewhat of an anomaly in that for the better part of my life, I have been a professional composer. I have written music for documentary films, art films, industrial-animated features, incidental music for the theater, TV specials and institutional commercials. Being the author of *Knowing the Score: Notes on Film Music,* I often lecture at universities on the subject, where my book is a standard text. And, I confess I play the horses. Now this may not seem like a dignified avocation for a serious artist, but upon occasion it has been a financial bonus. Being a professional has helped me in various ways, besides providing an alternative choice regarding making a living ... something that young composers should look into, especially if they do not want to teach, detest horses, do not have a source of income, or an outside profession, or haven't met and married a wealthy spouse. I learned to write music quickly (because I worked in the non-theatrical field, I was able to duplicate my concert style to a remarkable degree), have my music performed immediately by the best musicians in the world, and developed a technique for rehearsing and conducting an orchestra. Thus, when I happened to have the opportunity of conducting my own music with the Detroit, Louisville, Kansas City, National Symphonies and Orchestre National de Lille (France), I didn't fall flat on my face; I knew what I was doing.

Darius Milhaud used to say, "don't talk too much about your compositional techniques; a good cook doesn't give out his recipes." In this context, I admit I'm not much on program notes. Some composers write pages of notes for a piece often lasting only a few minutes, or in some cases, an eternity, by ascribing all kinds of philosophical connotations and heroic proportions to their work, qualities which are generally figments of their imagination. There are enough composers around practising the craft of artistic obfuscation without adding my name to the list. I have basically one set of program notes for every piece I write. Prominence of musical line depends on dynamics, impact-accents, phrasing, rhythmic propulsion, color, contrast and the general character of the music. There are certain 12-tone and jazz elements present, neither strict nor formal. And, the triplet is my musical heartbeat.

A composer spends a lifetime searching for his own sounds and sometimes when he finds them, he discovers they are not fashionable. I believe a composer cannot escape his roots. I have lived all my life in the big city. The rebellious mutterings, cross rhythms, nervous tension and energy, the beat of the city, are in my music, and contrary to popular opinion, you don't have to write pseudo-western music to be an American composer. You cannot have life without a pulse-beat, and for me, you cannot have music without rhythmic propulsion. And, I like to think I have a lot of rhythm for a white guy.

I am not a minimalist. My music will not create a slow hypnotic, soporific effect. If you want to be hypnotised, see a hypnotist. My music will not put you to sleep or in a trance. It is more akin to a hypodermic galvanizing needle. My slogan is not "simplify and repeat," it is "organise and invent."

While I have never regarded music as an artistic contest or competitive race - I always thought it was a love affair, a contract with life, a marriage - and after 50 years, I still do, I admit, at the danger of contradicting myself, that novelist Dawn Powell's line contains germs of truth and reality in 1990. She has written: "One has to keep running, because in the end, it is the only prize there is ... to be alive, to be in the race."

Thank you.

Chronological List of Works and First Performances

IB1. **Fugue for Piano**

In three voices.

Composed: March 1942. This date is given at the beginning of the score.

Publication: Bound by the Kayser Music Binding Company, Chicago.

Premiere: Unknown.

Manuscript: Library of Congress, Bazelon Collection, box J, ink on manuscript paper, 4 pp.

(1) There are inconsistencies in the score. Most of the score is in blue ink, possibly in a copyist's hand. There are some additions in black ink in Bazelon's hand.

(2) The additions are the composer's name, the date of composition, some dynamics, and an alteration to the part-writing of one passage.

IB2. **Double Fuga for String Quartet**

Composed: June 1942. This date is given at the beginning of the score.

Publication: Bound by the Kayser Music Binding Company, Chicago.

Premiere: Unknown.

Manuscript: Library of Congress, Bazelon Collection, box J, ink on manuscript paper, 6 pp.

(1) See note (1) under IB1.

(2) The additions are the composer's name, the date of composition, and some dynamics.

IB3. Ode to a New Day
First Poem for Orchestra
For picc 3 2 Ehn 2 bclt 2 cfg / 4 2 3 1 / timp perc hrp / strings.
Composed: June 1943.
Publication: Bound by the Kayser Music Binding Company, Chicago.
Premiere: Unknown.
Manuscript: Library of Congress, Bazelon Collection, box J, ink on
    manuscript paper, 35 pp.
(1) See note (1) under IB1.
(2) The additions are the composer's name, the date of composition, and
    the subtitle.

IB4. Humouresque for Orchestra
Comic Overture
For picc 3 (3: picc2) 2 2 (in A) Dclt 2 cfg / 4 2 3 1 / timp pno/xyl hrp /
    strings.
Composed: January 1944.
Publication: Bound by the Kayser Music Binding Company, Chicago.
Premiere: School of Music, DePaul University, Chicago, January 1944;
    Magdalen Massmann and Shirley Effenbach (version for two pianos).
Manuscript: Library of Congress, Bazelon Collection, box J, ink on
    manuscript paper, 58 pp. The version for two pianos has not survived.
(1) See note (1) under IB1.
(2) The additions are the composer's name, the date of composition, and
    some changes to the musical content.

IB5. Music for Violin
The words "Part I - Part II" also appear on the title page.
Composed: December 1944.
Publication: Reproduced and bound by the Kayser Music Binding
    Company, Chicago.
Premiere: Unknown.
Manuscript: Unknown. A copy of the original publication reproduced
    from the composer's manuscript is in the Library of Congress,
    Bazelon Collection, box J, 16 pp.

IB6. A Song Cycle
For Solo Alto, Violin, Cello, Clarinet in A and Piano
            1: Remember (Christina Rosetti)
            2: When I am Dead, my Dearest (Christina Rosetti)
            3: So Deep is Death (Frank Kendon)
Composed: February 1945.
Publication: Reproduced and bound by the Kayser Music Binding
    Company, Chicago.

Premiere: Unknown.

Manuscript: Unknown. A copy of the original publication reproduced from the composer's manuscript is in the Library of Congress, Bazelon Collection, box J, 11 pp.

IB7. Symphonic Variations on an Old English Folk Theme
Theme, Nine Variations and Finale
For orchestra: 3 (3:picc) 2 2 2 / 4 3 3 1 / timp 3perc pno / strings.
Composed: April 10, 1945.
Publication: Reproduced and bound probably by the Kayser Music Binding Company, Chicago.
Premiere: Unknown.
Manuscript: Unknown. A copy of the original publication reproduced from the composer's manuscript is in the Library of Congress, Bazelon Collection, box J, 86 pp.

IB8. String Quartet No. 1
Composed: May 15, 1945.
Publication: Bound by the Kayser Music Binding Company, Chicago.
Premiere: Unknown.
Manuscript: Library of Congress, Bazelon Collection, box J, ink on manuscript paper, 19 pp.

IB9. Suite for Piano No. 1
Composed: May 1945.
Publication: Reproduced and bound by the Kayser Music Publishing Company, Chicago.
Premiere: Unknown.
Manuscript: Unknown. A copy of the original publication reproduced from the composer's manuscript is in the Library of Congress, Bazelon Collection, box J, 7 pp.

IB10. Fantasia Contrapunctica
For Piano
Composed: June 2, 1945.
Publication: Bound by the Kayser Music Binding Company, Chicago.
Premiere: Unknown.
Manuscript: Library of Congress, Bazelon Collection, box J, ink on manuscript paper, 8 pp.

IB11. Elegy for String Orchestra
The score is marked "In Memoriam."
Composed: June 12, 1945.
Publication: Bound by the Kayser Music Binding Company, Chicago.

Premiere: Unknown.

Manuscript: Library of Congress, Bazelon Collection, box J, ink on manuscript paper, 6 pp.

IB12. Intermezzo No. 1 for Piano

Composed: September 1, 1945.

Publication: Bound by the Kayser Music Binding Company, Chicago.

Premiere: Unknown.

Manuscript: Library of Congress, Bazelon Collection, box J, ink on manuscript paper, 6 pp.

IB13. Praeludium for Piano

Composed: December 15, 1945.

Publication: Bound by the Kayser Music Binding Company, Chicago.

Premiere: Unknown.

Manuscript: Library of Congress, Bazelon Collection, box J, ink on manuscript paper, 5 pp.

IB14. Intermezzo No. 2 for Piano

Composed: December 25, 1945. Inscribed "written and completed on Christmas Day."

Publication: Bound by the Kayser Music Binding Company, Chicago.

Premiere: Unknown.

Manuscript: Library of Congress, Bazelon Collection, box J, ink on manuscript paper, 4 pp.

IB15. Orchestral Fantasy
Second Poem for Orchestra

For 3 2 2 2 / 4 2 3 1 / timp perc pno / strings.

Dedicated "to my mother."

Composed: 1945. The year of composition has been added in pencil to the ink title page.

Publication: Bound by the Kayser Music Binding Company, Chicago.

Premiere: Unknown.

Manuscript: Library of Congress, Bazelon Collection, box J, ink on manuscript paper, 58 pp.

IB16. Classical Scherzo
For String Orchestra and Timpani

Composed: June 1946.

Publication: Bound by the Kayser Music Binding Company, Chicago.

Premiere: Unknown.

Manuscript: Library of Congress, Bazelon Collection, box J, ink on manuscript paper, 28 pp.

IB17   Sonata No. 1 for Violin and Piano
   Composed: August 1946.
   Publication: Bound by the Kayser Music Binding Company, Chicago.
   Premiere: Unknown.
   Manuscript: Library of Congress, Bazelon Collection, box J, ink on
      manuscript paper, 29 pp.

IB18.   Trio for Flute, Oboe and Clarinet
   Composed: September 1946.
   Publication: Bound by the Kayser Music Binding Company, Chicago.
   Premiere: Unknown.
   Manuscript: Library of Congress, Bazelon Collection, box J, ink on
      manuscript paper, 19 pp.

IB19.   String Quartet No. 2
   Second Prize, National Federation of Music Clubs Competition, 1947.
   Composed: October - November 1946.
   Publication: Reproduced and bound, probably by Presto Reproductions,
      New York City, since they produced the parts.
   Premiere: Composer's Forum, McMillin Academic Theater, Columbia
      University, New York, October 23, 1948; New York String Quartet.
   Manuscript: Library of Congress, Bazelon Collection, box 1, ink on
      transparencies, 40 pp.

IB20.   Sonata No. 1 for Piano
   Composed: April 13, 1947, Mills College, Oakland, California.
   Revised: April 1952, New York City.
   Publication: Reproduced and bound by Independent Music Publishers,
      New York City. The company is not acknowledged on the front cover
      but its imprint is on each page.
   Premiere: League of Composers Concert, Museum of Modern Art, New
      York, February 8, 1948; Bernado Segall.
   Manuscript: Library of Congress, Bazelon Collection, box 1, ink on
      transparencies, 14 pp.

IB21.   Chamber Symphonette No. 1
   For chamber orchestra: 1 0 1 0 / 0 1 0 0 / - / strings.
   Dedicated to Darius Milhaud.
   Composed: May 1947, Mills College, Oakland, California.
   Publication: Reproduced and bound by the Kayser Music Binding
      Company, Chicago.
   Premiere: Belgium National Radio, Omroepcentrum, March 15, 1948;
      Kamerorkest en het Vlaams koor conducted by Jef Verelst.

Manuscript: Library of Congress, Bazelon Collection, box J, ink on transparencies, 16 pp.

IB22. Suite for Clarinet, Cello and Piano
Dedicated "to my teacher Darius Milhaud."

Composed: August 5, 1947, Mills College, Oakland, California.

Publication: Reproduced and bound by the Kayser Music Binding Company, Chicago. The company is not named on the score but the binding is the same as IB21.

Premiere: Composers' Forum, McMillin Academic Theater, Columbia University, New York, October 23, 1948; Abraham Nathanson, clarinet; Aaron Shapinsky, cello; Hilda Fenya, piano.

Manuscript: Library of Congress, Bazelon Collection, box J, ink on transparencies, 19 pp.

IB23. Three Preludes for Piano
Composed: September 1947, Oakland, California.

Publication: Reproduced and bound by Independent Music Publishers, New York City.

Premiere: Unknown.

Manuscript: Library of Congress, Bazelon Collection, box J, 4 pp.

(1) The manuscript of the score has been mounted (using staples and Scotch tape) on top of a reproduced copy.

IB24. Intermezzo No. 3
For piano.

Dedicated to Charles Jones.

Composed: October 8, 1947.

Publication: Reproduced and bound by the Kayser Music Binding Company, Chicago.

Premiere: Unknown.

Manuscript: Unknown. A copy of the original publication reproduced from the composer's manuscript is in the Library of Congress, Bazelon Collection, box J, 4 pp.

IB25. Adagio and Fugue
For String Orchestra
Composed: (1947). The date of composition is given in various catalogues, some of which were produced during Bazelon's lifetime.

Publication: Weintraub Music Company, New York, 1956.

Premiere: Not yet performed.

Manuscript: The printed miniature score is a reproduction from the composer's manuscript. A copy of the score is in the Library of Congress, Bazelon Collection, box 31, 15 pp.

IB26. Serenade for Piano

Composed: (1947?).

Publication: Unpublished.

Premiere: Unknown.

Manuscript: Library of Congress, Bazelon Collection, box J, 4 pp and 7 pp.

The manuscript exists in two formats. One is on an unusual pale green manuscript paper with a title page and four pages of music numbered 1-4. The other is the same music, on transparencies, with a title page, but the first page of music is labelled II and the seven pages of music are numbered 15-21.

IB27. Woodwind Quartet

For flute, oboe, clarinet in B flat and bassoon.

Composed: (1947). The score is undated. "?47" has been added in pencil. The manuscript and binding are similar to IB23 (September 1947).

Publication: Reproduced and bound by Independent Music Publishers, New York City.

Premiere: Unknown.

Manuscript: Library of Congress, Bazelon Collection, box J, ink on transparencies, 23 pp.

IB28. Concerto - Symphonique

For piano and orchestra: 3 (3:picc) 2 2 bclt 2 / 4 2 3 1 / timp / strings.

Composed: The piano reduction is dated June 1, 1948, New York City. The full score is undated.

Publication: Unpublished.

Premiere: Not yet performed.

Manuscript: Library of Congress, Bazelon Collection, box J, ink on transparencies, 119 pp.

IB29. Three Abstractions (Ballet - Suite)

For flute, saxophone (bass clarinet), bassoon, trumpet, piano, and optional percussion.

Composed for Valerie Bettis.

The title *It Is Always Farewell,* under which name the work was performed, has been added to the title page of the score.

Composed: August 10, 1948, New York City.

Publication: Bound by Presto Reproductions, New York City.

Premiere: American Dance Festival, Palmer Auditorium, Connecticut College, New London, Connecticut, August 18, 1949; Valerie Bettis Company.

Manuscript: Library of Congress, Bazelon Collection, box J, ink on manuscript paper, 22 pp.

IB30. Four Symphonic Episodes for Orchestra
For 2 2 2 2 / 2 2 0 0 / timp pno / strings.
Dedicated to Madeline Milhaud.
Composed: February 1949.
Publication: Reproduced and bound by Presto Reproductions, New York City.
Premiere: Not yet performed.
Manuscript: Library of Congress, Bazelon Collection, box J, ink on transparencies, 68 pp.

IB31. Sonatine for Piano
Composed: March 14, 1949, New York City.
Revised: Material from this work was later used in the composition of **Vignette**, IB66, in 1975.
Publication: Unpublished.
Premiere: Unknown.
Manuscript: Library of Congress, Bazelon Collection, box J, ink on transparencies, 9 pp.

IB32. Sonata No. 2 for Piano
Composed: June - August 1949, E. MacDowell Colony, Peterboro, New Hampshire.
Revised: April 1952, New York City.
Publication: Reproduced and bound by Independent Music Publishers, New York City. The company is not acknowledged on the front cover but its imprint is on each page.
Premiere: ISCM Forum Group, Dalcroze Auditorium, New York City, March 17, 1950; Marga Richter.
Manuscript: Library of Congress, Bazelon Collection, box 1, ink on transparencies, 21 pp.

IB33. Winter Wake
Ballet Solo
For piano, dancer and voice narration.
Text by Phoebe Pierce, *Winter in the Asylum*.
Dedicated to and written for Andora Hodgin.
Composed: October 10 - 20, 1949, New York City.
Publication: Bound by Independent Music Publishers, New York City.
Premiere: Unknown.
Manuscript: Library of Congress, Bazelon Collection, box J, ink on manuscript paper, 11 pp.

IB34. Sonata for Violin and Piano

The work should be named no. 2 to distinguish it from IB17.

One copy was dedicated to Manuel Wilk but the dedication has been partially erased.

Composed: (1949?). The dating of this piece is based on similarities between its paper and binding and other dated works from this period.

Publication: Reproduced and bound by Presto Reproductions, New York City.

Premiere: Unknown.

Manuscript: Unknown. A copy of the original publication reproduced from the composer's manuscript is in the Library of Congress, Bazelon Collection, box J, 28 pp.

IB35. Five Pieces for Violoncello and Piano

Composed: April 1950, New York City.

Publication: Weintraub Music Company, New York, 1956.

Premiere: Composers Concordance, Bernard Mayer Auditorium, The New School for Social Research, New York City, April 4, 1988; Amanda Forsyth, cello; Faine Wright, piano.

Manuscript: Unknown. A copy of the published score of the work is in the Library of Congress, Bazelon Collection, box 31, 14 pp.

IB36. Five Pieces for Piano

Dedicated to Ruth.

Composed: June 1950, Peterboro, New Hampshire.

Publication: Weintraub Music Company, New York City, 1956.

Premiere: ISCM, McMillin Theater, Columbia University, April 1, 1951; Ruth Strassman.

Manuscript: Unknown. A copy of the published score of the work is in the Library of Congress, Bazelon Collection, box 31, 10 pp.

IB37A. Ten Orchestral Pieces for Young People

For 2 (2:picc) 2 (2:Ehn) 2 (2:bclt) 2 / 2 2 1 0 / timp 2perc pno / strings.

    1. Prelude
    2. Dance for a Tomboy
    3. Lullaby
    4. The Clown and the Puppet
    5. Cowboy Tune
    6. The Haunted Chateau
    7. Circus Parade
    8. Christmas Carol
    9. Goblins and Ghosts
    10. Prayer

Composed: 1950, New York City.

Publication: Bound by Independent Music Publishers, New York City.
Premiere: Not yet performed.
Manuscript: Library of Congress, Bazelon Collection, box J, ink on manuscript paper, 70 pp.

IB37B. Suite for Young People
For Piano
Published in two parts.

Part one is dedicated to Mother and Dad.

Part two is dedicated to Ruth.

An arrangement of IB37A for piano with two movements (part one: 1, part two: 5) added.

Part One
   1. Little Serenade
   2. Christmas Carol
   3. Dance for a Tomboy
   4. Lullaby
   5. Cowboy Tune
   6. Prayer

Part Two
   1. Prelude
   2. The Clown and the Puppet
   3. Circus Parade
   4. The Haunted Chateau
   5. Dance of an Elf
   6. Goblins and Ghosts

Composed: (1950).

Publication: Peer International Corporation, New York, 1954.
   Part One: 287-8, Part Two: 288-17.

Premiere: Four pieces from the Suite: Dance of a Tomboy, Cowboy Song, Christmas Carol, Circus Parade were included in a recital given in Town Hall, New York City, October 16, 1950; Ruth Strassman.

Manuscript: Unknown. Copies of the printed scores are in the Library of Congress, Bazelon Collection, box 31, Part One: 10 pp. Part Two: 19 pp.

IB38. Suite for Small Orchestra
Adapted from material originally written as film music for a documentary for Girl-Scouts of America and initially called **The Growing Years, Suite for Small Orchestra.**

Composed: January 1951. This date is given on the first version of the work.

Publication: Weintraub Music Company, New York City, 1956.

Premiere: Not yet performed.

Manuscript: Unknown. The printed miniature score is a reproduction of the composer's manuscript. A copy of the score is in the Library of Congress, Bazelon Collection, box 32, 65 pp. The first version of the work, **The Growing Years**, is in the Library of Congress, Bazelon Collection, box 29, 62 pp.

IB39. Sonatina for Piano

Dedicated to Dr. Kurt A. Adler.

Composed: April 1952, New York City.

Publication: Weintraub Music Company, New York City, 1954.

Premiere: Carnegie Recital Hall, New York City, January 15, 1989; Faine Wright.

Manuscript: Unknown. A copy of the published score is in the Library of Congress, Bazelon Archive, box 32.

IB40. Sonata No. 3 for Piano
(In one movement)

Dedicated to William Masselos.

Composed: May 1952, New York City.

Publication: Reproduced and bound by Independent Music Publishers, New York City.

Premiere: MacDowell Colony Composers' Festival, Hartt College College of Music, Hartford, Connecticut, November 23, 1953; Madelyn Robb.

Manuscript: Library of Congress, Bazelon Collection, box 1, ink on transparencies, 11 pp.

IB41. Concert Overture

For orchestra: 3 (3:picc) 2 Ehn 2 bclt 2 cfg / 4 3 3 1 / timp 3perc pno / strings.

Dedicated to Dr. Irving Harris.

Composed: 1951 - 1952, New York City.

Revised: 1961. The date of composition given on the revised score is 1952, New York City.

Woodwind revised to: picc 2 2 Ehn 2 (1:Eclt) bclt 2 /.

Publication: Weintraub Music Company, 1956. Revised version: Theodore Presser Company: rental.

Premiere: Carnegie Hall, New York City, March 21, 1965; Orchestra of America conducted by Richard Korn.

Manuscript: The miniature score printed by Weintraub is a reproduction of the composer's manuscript. This manuscript is in the Library of Congress, Bazelon Collection, box 3, pencil on transparencies, 68 pp. The revised version exists in the form of emendations to a published score in the composer's estate.

IB42. Movimento da Camera
For Flute, Bassoon, Horn and Harpsichord
Composed: November 1954.
Revised: May 1960.
Publication: Theodore Presser Company: rental.
Premiere: Associated American Artists Galleries, New York City, December 11, 1954: New Art Wind Quintet.
Manuscript: Library of Congress, Bazelon Collection, box 2, pencil on transparencies, 27 pp.

IB43. In Dulci Jubilo
For unaccompanied SATB chorus.
Composed: (1955).
Publication: Six Famous Carols arranged by Three Young Americans, Performers Library Inc., Washington D.C., 1955.
Premiere: There is no record of a performance in the 1950s. The work was performed in St Fin Barre's Cathedral, Cork, Republic of Ireland, December 18, 1997; Choir of University College Cork conducted by David Harold Cox.
Manuscript: Unknown. A copy of the published score is in the Library of Congress, Bazelon Collection, box 32, 2 pp.

IB44. Chamber Concerto No. 1 for Eight Players
For flute (piccolo), clarinet (E flat clarinet), trumpet, tuba, violin, piano and two percussionists.
Originally entitled **Sound Track for Seven Piece Set** then renamed **Chamber Symphony for Seven Instruments.**
Commissioned by the New York Philharmonic Ensemble.
Composed: Xmas, 1956, New York City.
Publication: Theodore Presser Company: rental.
Premiere: 92nd Street YMHA, New York City, January 20, 1957; New York Philharmonic Chamber Ensemble conducted by the composer.
Manuscript: Library of Congress, Bazelon Collection, box 1, ink on transparencies, 46 pp.

IB45. Suite from Shakespeare's "The Merry Wives of Windsor"
For orchestra: 1 (:picc) 1 1 (:Eclt) 1 / 2 2 0 1 / 2perc pno / vla vcl.
Adapted from incidental music written for a production of Shakespeare's *The Merry Wives of Windsor* in 1959.
Composed: January 1960, New York City.
Publication: Theodore Presser Company: rental.
Premiere: Not yet performed.
Manuscript: Library of Congress, Bazelon Collection, box 2, pencil on transparencies, 98 pp.

IB46. Overture to a Comedy
(Shakespeare's "The Taming of the Shrew")
For orchestra: 1 (:picc) 1 1 (:Eclt) 1 / timp 3perc pno / strings.
Adapted from the overture written for a production of Shakespeare's *The Taming of the Shrew* in 1957.
The work subsequently became known as:
Overture to Shakespeare's "The Taming of the Shrew"
Composed: May 1960, New York City.
Revised: May 1969, New York City.
Publication: Theodore Presser Company: rental.
Premiere: National Gallery of Art, Washington D.C., May 24, 1964; National Gallery Orchestra conducted by Richard Bales.
Manuscript: Library of Congress, Bazelon Collection, box 4, pencil on transparencies, 77 pp.

IB47. Concert Ballet: Centauri 17
For ensemble: 1 1 1 (:Eclt) bcl 1 / 1 2 0 1 / theremin (or lyric soprano) timp 3perc pno / vla vlc.
Composed: (1959).
Publication: Theodore Presser Company: rental.
Premiere: Not yet publicly performed. The work was recorded privately by Bazelon on November 13, 1959.
Manuscript: Library of Congress, Bazelon Collection, box 2, ink on transparencies, 69 pp.

IB48. Symphony No. 1
(In one movement)
For orchestra: picc 2 2 Ehn 2 (1:Eclt) bclt 2 / 4 3 3 1 / timp 4perc pno cel / strings.
Composed: August 1960 - February 1961, New York City.
Publication: Theodore Presser Company: rental.
Premiere: Music Hall, Kansas City, Missouri, October 26, 1963; Kansas City Philharmonic conducted by Hans Schwieger.
Manuscript: Library of Congress, Bazelon Collection, box 2, ink on transparencies, 158 pp.

IB49. Short Symphony
Testament To A Big City
The numbering Bazelon used for his symphonies shows that he regarded this as his second symphony.
For orchestra: 2 (1&2: picc) 2 2 (1:Eclt, 2:bclt) 2 / 2 (+2 opt.) 3 2 1 / timp 3perc pno/cel / strings.
Originally subtitled **Testimonial To A Big City** (1962) then **Testimony To A Big City** (1966).

Dedicated to Howard Mitchell.

Composed: December 1961, New York City.

Publication: Boosey and Hawkes, F.S.326, 1967.

Premiere: Constitution Hall, Washington D.C., December 4, 1962; National Symphony Orchestra conducted by the composer.

Manuscript: Library of Congress, Bazelon Collection, box 3 (pencil on transparencies), 69 pp.

IB50. Symphony No. 3

For Brass, Percussion, Piano and Sextet

For 0 0 0 0 / 4 6 4 2 / 4perc pno cel / - / and a sextet of flute and piccolo, two clarinets (E flat and bass), electric guitar, viola and cello.

Composed: May - September 1962, New York City.

Publication: Theodore Presser Company: rental.

Premiere: Not yet performed.

Manuscript: Library of Congress, Bazelon Collection, box 3, ink on transparencies, 164 pp.

IB51. Brass Quintet

For two trumpets in C, horn, tenor and bass trombones.

Commissioned by the American Brass Quintet.

Composed: May - June 1963, New York City.

Publication: Boosey and Hawkes, B. Ens. 145, 1965.

Premiere: Kaufmann Concert Hall, New York City, March 22, 1964; American Brass Quintet.

Manuscript: Score: unknown. Parts: reproductions of the composer's manuscript. A copy of the score is in the Library of Congress, Bazelon Collection, box 31, 40 pp.

IB52. Duo for Viola and Piano

Dedicated to Karen Phillips and Glenn Jacobson.

Composed: (1963).

Revised: December 1970, New York City.

The score is dated December 1970 but the work was performed in 1964.

Publication: Novello, 12 0536 06, 1981, now available from Theodore Presser Company.

Premiere: Artists Choice Concert, New School for Social Research, New York City, March 20, 1964; Karen Tuttle, viola; Mitchie Tashijan, piano. The premiere of the revised version was given in the Mohawk Trail Concert Series, Charlemont, Massachusetts, August 4, 1973; Karen Phillips, viola; Glenn Jacobson, piano.

Manuscript: The printed score is a reproduction of the composer's manuscript. The original is in the Library of Congress, Bazelon Collection, box 6, pencil on transparencies, 24 pp.

IB53. Symphony No. 4

For orchestra: picc 2 (2:picc) 2 Ehn 2 Eclt bclt 2 cfg / 4 3 3 1 / timp 5perc pno cel / strings.

Composed: August 1964 - April 1965, New York City.

Publication: Theodore Presser Company: rental.

Premiere: Not yet publicly performed, recorded in 1999 on Albany Records CD Troy 370, Rousse Philharmonic conducted by Harold Farberman.

Manuscript: Library of Congress, Bazelon Collection, box 4, pencil on transparencies, 208 pp.

IB53A. Dramatic Movement for Orchestra

This work is the first movement of **Symphony No. 4**. It was given its own title and performed, so Bazelon clearly felt it could stand on its own as an integral piece of music.

Composed: (August 1964 - April 1965) Scores of the Dramatic Movement are not dated.

Publication: Reproduced and bound by Independent Music Publishers, New York City, now available on rental from Theodore Presser Company.

Premiere: Opera House, Seattle, Washington, February 21, 1966; Seattle Symphony conducted by Milton Katims.

Manuscript: The score of Symphony No. 4 in the Library of Congress, Bazelon Collection, box 4, pencil on transparencies, 112 pp.

IB53B. Two Movements for Orchestra

This work is the second and third movements of **Symphony No. 4**. It was renamed and re-dated. Bazelon presumably would have therefore approved its performance but would no doubt have preferred that the symphony should be played in its entirety.

Composed: August 1967 - April 1968, New York City. The dates that appear at the end of **Symphony No. 4** have been altered to give a new date of composition.

Publication: Reproduced and bound by Independent Music Publishers, New York City.

Premiere: Not yet performed.

Manuscript: The score of Symphony No. 4 in the Library of Congress, Bazelon Collection, box 4, pencil on transparencies, 96 pp.

IB54. Excursion for Orchestra

The work is also sometimes referred to as **Excursions**.

For: picc 2 2 Ehn 2 Eclt 2 cfg / 4 3 3 1 / timp 4perc pno / strings.

Dedicated to Hans Schwieger.

Composed: November 1965, New York City.

Publication: Reproduced and bound by Independent Music Publishers, New York City, now available from Theodore Presser Company: rental.

Premiere: Music Hall, Kansas City, Missouri, March 29, 1966; Kansas City Philharmonic conducted by Hans Schwieger. This performance was originally scheduled for March 1, 1966 but postponed due to illness in the percussion section.

Manuscript: Library of Congress, Bazelon Collection, box 4, pencil on transparencies, 87 pp.

IB55. Early American Suite
For Wind Quintet and Harpsichord
Composed: November - December 1965, New York City.
Publication: Theodore Presser Company, 114 - 40866, 1997.
Premiere: Not yet performed.
Manuscript: Library of Congress, Bazelon Collection, box 4, pencil on transparencies, 59 pp.

IB56. Idea and Elaboration
For Orchestra
For: picc 2 2 Ehn 2 Eclt bclt 2 cfg / 4 3 3 1 / timp 5perc pno / strings.
This work was renamed **Spirits of the Night** in 1976.
Composed: October 1, 1966, New York City.
Publication: Reproduced and bound by Independent Music Publishers, New York City.
Premiere: Not yet performed.
Manuscript: Library of Congress, Bazelon Collection (as altered to become **Spirits of the Night**), box 6, pencil on transparencies, 69 pp.

IB57. Symphony No. 5
For orchestra: picc 2 2 Ehn 2 Eclt bclt 2 cfg / 4 3 3 1 / timp 5perc pno / strings.
Dedicated to Izler Solomon and the Indianapolis Symphony Orchestra.
Composed: February 1967, New York City.
Publication: Boosey and Hawkes, F.S.399, 1973.
Premiere: Clowes Memorial Hall, Indianapolis, Indiana, May 8, 1969; Indianapolis Symphony Orchestra conducted by Izler Solomon.
Manuscript: Library of Congress, Bazelon Collection, box 5, pencil on transparencies, 118 pp.

IB57A. Mohawk Trail Fanfare
For brass (1 2 1 1) and timpani (optional).
Adapted from the beginning and the end of the fourth movement of **Symphony No. 5**.

Composed: (1980). The adaptation contains a notational element only found in Bazelon's work after 1972.

Publication: Theodore Presser Company: rental.

Premiere: Mohawk Trail Concert Series, Charlemont, Massachusetts, July 5, 1980, Berkshire East Orchestral Pops Orchestra conducted by Abba Bogin.

Manuscript: Library of Congress, Bazelon Collection, box 6, pencil on transparencies, 3 pp.

IB58. Symphony Concertante
For Clarinet, Trumpet, Marimba and Orchestra

For: picc 2 2 1 Ecl bcl 2 / 4 3 3 1 / timp 4-5perc pno / strings.

Composed: December 1968, New York City.

Publication: Theodore Presser Company, 416-41136, 1995.

Premiere: Chapin Hall, Williams College, Williamstown, Massachusetts, April 26, 1985; Berkshire Symphony Orchestra conducted by Julius Heygi; Susan Martula, clarinet; Paul Sunderberg, trumpet; Richard Albagli, marimba.

Manuscript: The printed score is a reproduction of the composer's manuscript. The original is in the Library of Congress, Bazelon Collection, box 5, pencil on transparencies, 138 pp.

IB59. Symphony No. 6

For orchestra: picc 2 2 Eclt 2 bclt 2 cfg / 4 3 3 1 / timp 5perc accord / ten rec / strings.

This work was based on music written for the TV documentary *Survival 67* and was given the title **Symphony No. Six-Day War** for its first performance.

Composed: June - December 1969, New York City.

Publication: Theodore Presser Company: rental.

Premiere: Music Hall, Kansas City, Missouri, November 17, 1970; Kansas City Philharmonic conducted by the composer.

Manuscript: Library of Congress, Bazelon Collection, box 5, pencil on transparencies, 111 pp.

IB60. Dramatic Fanfare for 1970

For brass (4 3 2 0) and percussion (3perc).

Winner of the Cleveland Orchestra Blossom Music Center Fanfare Competition, 1970.

Composed: (1970). There is no date at the end of the score.

Publication: Boosey and Hawkes: rental.

Premiere: Blossom Music Center, Ohio, summer 1970, Cleveland Orchestra conducted by Louis Lane.

Manuscript: Library of Congress, Bazelon Collection, box 6, pencil and ink on manuscript paper, 6 pp.

IB61. Churchill Downs
Chamber Concerto No. 2

For one solo woodwind (alto saxophone + clarinet + flute or piccolo) and thirteen players: horn, three trumpets, two trombones, electric guitar, electric bass guitar (Fender) and string bass, electric organ, electric piano, three percussionists.

Commissioned by Max Pollikoff, for the Music In Our Time series.

Composed: July 1970 - February 1971, New York City.

Publication: Boosey and Hawkes, F.S.228, 1977.

Premiere: Music In Our Time series, 92nd Street YMHA, New York City, October 16, 1971; chamber ensemble conducted by the composer.

Manuscript: The location of the original manuscript is unknown. The printed score is a reproduction of the composer's manuscript. A copy of the printed score is in the Library of Congress, Bazelon Collection, box 31, 86 pp.

IB62. Phenomena
For Voice and Chamber Ensemble

For: 1 (:picc) 1 2 (1:Eclt) bclt 1 (:cfg) / 1 1 1 0 / 2perc pno ("tacky barroom upright") / strings 1 0 1 1 1.

Composed: May - August 1972, New York City - Sagaponack, Long Island.

Publication: Theodore Presser Company: rental.

Premiere: Not yet performed.

Manuscript: Library of Congress, Bazelon Collection, box 6, pencil on transparencies, 69 pp.

IB63. Propulsions
Concerto for Percussion

For an ensemble of seven percussionists playing a wide variety of western, eastern and African instruments.

Dedicated to Herb Harris.

Composed: May 1974, New York City.

Publication: Boosey and Hawkes, F.S.430, 1978.

Premiere: Alice Tully Hall, Lincoln Center, New York City, April 27, 1975; Brooklyn College Percussion Ensemble conducted by Morris Lang. The work had been recorded prior to this performance.

Manuscript: Unknown. A copy of the printed score is in the Library of Congress, Bazelon Collection, box 31, 54 pp.

IB64. Woodwind Quintet
For Flute, Oboe, Clarinet, Horn and Bassoon
Commissioned by the Boehm Woodwind Quintette.
Composed: February 1975, New York City.
Publication: Novello, 09 0563, 01, 1982, now available from Theodore Presser Company.
Premiere: Alice Tully Hall, New York City, May 22, 1975; Boehm Woodwind Quintette.
Manuscript: The location of the original is unknown. The printed score is a reproduction of the composer's manuscript. A copy of the printed score is in the Library of Congress, Bazelon Collection, box 32, 58 pp.

IB65. A Quiet Piece . . . for a Violent Time
For orchestra: picc 1 (:alto) 1 1 bclt 1 / 3 2 2 1 / 3perc hp / strings.
Dedicated to Werner Torkanowsky and the New Orleans Symphony Orchestra.
Composed: June 1975, New York City.
Publication: Boosey and Hawkes, F.S.429, 1977.
Premiere: New Orleans Theater of the Performing Arts, New Orleans, Louisiana, October 28, 1975; New Orleans Philharmonic Symphony Orchestra conducted by Werner Torkanowsky.
Manuscript: The location of the original is unknown. The printed score is a reproduction of the composer's manuscript. A copy of the printed score is in the Library of Congress, Bazelon Collection, box 31, 40 pp.

IB66. Vignette
For harpsichord.
Composed: (1975). The work was written with a specific occasion in mind but not performed at that time.
Publication: Theodore Presser Company, 110-40717, 1996.
Premiere: Not yet publicly performed, recorded in 1998 on Albany Records CD Troy 282 by John Van Buskirk.
Manuscript: Library of Congress, Bazelon Collection, box 6, pencil on transparencies, 8 pp.

IB67. Double Crossings
Duo for Trumpet and Percussion
Commissioned by Morris Lang and Gerard Schwarz.
Composed: February 1976, New York City.
Publication: Boosey and Hawkes, B.W.I.266, 1978.
Double Premiere: Carnegie Recital Hall, New York City, December 5, 1976; Gerard Schwarz, trumpet; Morris Lang, percussion. Brown

Hall, The New England Conservatory of Music, Boston, Massachusetts, December 5, 1976; Rolf Smedvig, trumpet; Frank Epstein, percussion.

Manuscript: Unknown. A copy of the printed score is in the Library of Congress, Bazelon Collection, box 31, 21 pp.

IB68. Concatenations
For Percussion Quartet and Viola

Commissioned by Frank Epstein.

Composed: June 1976, New York City.

Publication: Theodore Presser Company: rental.

Premiere: Jordan Hall, New England Conservatory of Music, Boston, Massachusetts, May 1, 1977; New England Conservatory of Music Percussion Ensemble conducted by Frank Epstein; Burton Fine, viola.

Manuscript: Library of Congress, Bazelon Collection, boxes 6, pencil on transparencies, incomplete, and 18, photocopy, 51 pp.

IB69. Spirits of the Night
(Sound Dreams)

For orchestra: picc 2 2 Ehn 2 Eclt bclt 2 cfg / 4 3 3 1 / timp 5perc pno / strings.

The first version of this work was written in 1966 and called **Idea and Elaboration**. In addition to the change of title, Bazelon made a few alterations to the score, mostly concerned with phrasing.

Composed: October 1, 1976, New York City.

Publication: Theodore Presser Company: rental.

Premiere: Not yet performed.

Manuscript: Library of Congress, Bazelon Collection, box 6, pencil on transparencies, 69 pp.

IB70. De-Tonations
For Brass Quintet and Orchestra

For: picc 2 2 2 Eclt bclt 2 cfg / 3 2 2 1 / timp 4perc pno / strings.

Written for the American Brass Quintet with support from the National Endowment for the Arts.

Composed: December 1976, New York City.

Publication: Novello, 89 0118 10, 1982, now available from Theodore Presser Company.

Premiere: Carnegie Hall, New York City, April 3, 1979; American Brass Quintet and the National Orchestra of New York conducted by David Stahl.

Manuscript: The location of the original is unknown. The printed score is a reproduction of the composer's manuscript. A copy of the printed score is in the Library of Congress, Bazelon Collection, box 31, 61 pp.

IB71. Triple Play
For Two Trombones and Solo Percussion
Composed: March 1977, New York City.
Publication: Theodore Presser Company: rental.
Premiere: University of Sheffield, England, March 11, 1982; University of Sheffield Ensemble conducted by David Harold Cox.
Manuscript: Library of Congress, Bazelon Collection, box 6, pencil on transparencies, 23 pp.

IB72. Sound Dreams
For Chamber Ensemble
For flute, clarinet, viola, cello, piano, and solo percussion.
Commissioned by the Collage New Music Chamber Ensemble.
Written in memory of James Jones. The title page includes a quotation from James Jones: 'You composers live in a world of Sound Dreams.'
Composed: July 1977, New York City.
Publication: Novello, 89 0123 06, 1983, now available from Theodore Presser Company.
Premiere: Museum of Fine Arts, Boston, Massachusetts, November 13, 1977; Collage New Music Chamber Ensemble conducted by Gunther Schuller.
Manuscript: The printed score is a reproduction of the composer's manuscript. The original is in the Library of Congress, Bazelon Collection, box 6, pencil on transparencies, 36 pp.

IB73. Cross-Currents
For Brass Quintet and Solo Percussion
Commissioned by the Empire Brass Quintet.
Composed: February 1978, New York City.
Publication: Novello, 12 0571 04, 1983, now available from Theodore Presser Company.
Premiere: Sanders Theater, Cambridge, Massachusetts, January 16, 1981; Empire Brass Quintet; Frank Epstein, percussion.
Manuscript: The location of the original is unknown. The printed score is a reproduction of the composer's manuscript. A copy of the work is in the Library of Congress, Bazelon Collection, box 31, 48 pp.

IB74. Imprints . . . on Ivory and Strings
For Piano
Commissioned by and dedicated to Rebecca LaBrecque.

Composed: August 1978, New York City.

Publication: Novello, 10 0231 07, 1982, now available from Theodore Presser Company.

Premiere: Brown Hall, The New England Conservatory of Music, Boston, Massachusetts, January 30, 1979; Rebecca LaBrecque. A performance by Rebecca LaBrecque in Carnegie Recital Hall, New York City, February 10, 1979, was also described as a world premiere.

Manuscript: The printed score is a reproduction of the composer's manuscript. The original is in the Library of Congress, Bazelon Collection, box 6, ink on transparencies, 25 pp.

IB75. Three Men on a Dis-Course
For B flat Clarinet, Cello and Solo Percussion
Commissioned by Meyer Kupferman.

Composed: May 1979, New York City.

Publication: Theodore Presser Company: rental.

Premiere: Carnegie Recital Hall, New York City, April 9, 1980; Meyer Kupferman, clarinet; David Moore, cello; Jeff Kraus, percussion.

Manuscript: Unknown. A copy of the work, produced from the composer's manuscript, is in the Library of Congress, Bazelon Collection, box 18, 9 pp.

IB76. Junctures for Orchestra
For: picc 2 2 Ehn 2 bclt 2 cfg / 4 3 3 1 / timp 4perc pno/cel hp / strings.

Composed: October 1979, New York City.

Publication: Theodore Presser Company: rental.

Premiere: Not yet performed.

Manuscript: Unknown. A copy of the work, produced from the composer's manuscript, is in the Library of Congress, Bazelon Collection, box 18, 69 pp.

IB77. Partnership
For Timpani and Marimba
Commissioned by Jonathan Hass and William Moersch.

Composed: January 1980, New York City.

Publication: Novello, 12 0547 01, 1982, now available from Theodore Presser Company.

Premiere: Philadelphia Art Alliance, 251 South Eighteenth Street, Philadelphia, Pennsylvania; March 16, 1980; Jonathan Hass, timpani; William Moersch, marimba.

Manuscript: The printed score is a reproduction of the composer's manuscript. The original is in the Library of Congress, Bazelon Collection, box 7, pencil on transparencies, 21 pp.

IB78. Symphony No. 7

... in Two Parts (Ballet for Orchestra)

For: picc 2 2 2 Eclt bclt 2 cfg / 4 3 3 1 / timp 4perc ampl pno / strings.

Composed: October 1980, New York City.

Publication: Theodore Presser Company, 416-41146, 1996.

Premiere: Not yet publicly performed, recorded in 1995 on Albany Records CD Troy 174, Bournemouth Symphony Orchestra conducted by Harold Farberman.

Manuscript: The printed score is a reproduction of the composer's manuscript. The original is in the Library of Congress, Bazelon Collection, box 7, pencil on paper mounted on paper, 74 pp.

IB79. Suite for Marimba

Commissioned by and dedicated to William Moersch.

Composed: November 1980, New York City. The printed score bears two dates. The first of these, 1984, which appears in brackets under the composer's name at the beginning of the work, is incorrect. The correct date appears in the usual place at the end of the work.

Publication: Novello, 12 0678, 1989, now available from Theodore Presser Company.

Premiere: Christ and St. Stephen's Church, New York City, January 15, 1984; William Moersch.

Manuscript: Unknown. The printed score is a reproduction of the composer's manuscript. A copy of the work is in the Library of Congress, Bazelon Collection, box 32, 9 pp.

IB80. Memories of a Winter Childhood

For Orchestra

For: picc 2 1 Ehn 2 bclt 2 cfg / 4 3 3 1 / timp 4perc pno/cel hp / strings.

Composed: May 1981, New York City.

Publication: Theodore Presser Company, 416-41131, 1993, 1994.

Premiere: Harrisburg, Pennsylvania, December 5, 1989; Harrisburg Symphony Orchestra conducted by Larry Newland.

Manuscript: Library of Congress, Bazelon Collection, box 8, pencil on manuscript paper, 55 pp.

IB81. Spires ...

Concert Piece for Trumpet and Small Orchestra

For: 2 (2:picc) 2 (2:Ehn) 2 (2:bclt) 2 (2:cfg) / 2 1 1 0 / 2perc pno / strings 8 7 5 4 2.

Composed: December 1981, New York City.

Publication: Theodore Presser Company, 416-41127, 1992.

Premiere: Lille, France, February 6, 1989; Orchestre Philharmonique de Lille conducted by Harold Farberman; Dennis Hu, trumpet.

Manuscript: The printed score is a reproduction of the composer's manuscript. The original is in the Library of Congress, Bazelon Collection, box 8, pencil on manuscript paper, 54 pp.

IB82. Tides
For Solo Clarinet and Selected Instruments
For: 2 (1:picc, 2:afl) 1 asax 0 bcl 1 / 3 2 2 0 / 2perc hp / 0 0 6 4 2.
Composed: July 1982, New York City.
Publication: Theodore Presser Company: rental.
Premiere: Not yet performed.
Manuscript: Library of Congress, Bazelon Collection, box 9, pencil on paper, 78 pp.

IB83. Re-Percussions
For Two Pianos
Commissioned by Richard Rodney Bennett and John Philips.
Composed: November 1982, New York City.
Publication: Novello, 12 0279, 1987, now available from Theodore Presser Company.
Premiere: Guzzetta Recital Hall, University of Akron, Akron, Ohio, February 9, 1983; Richard Rodney Bennett and John Philips.
Manuscript: Library of Congress, Bazelon Collection, box 9, pencil on manuscript paper, 27 pp.

IB84. For Tuba . . . with Strings Attached
For tuba and string quartet (or string orchestra).
Commissioned by Harvey Phillips.
Composed: December 1982, New York City.
Publication: Theodore Presser Company: rental.
Premiere: Carnegie Recital Hall, New York City, January 10, 1985; Harvey Phillips, tuba; Laurentian String Quartet.
Manuscript: Library of Congress, Bazelon Collection, box 9, pencil on manuscript paper, 22 pp.

IB85. Fusions
For Chamber Ensemble
For picc 1 1 Ehn 1 bclt 1 / 1 2 1 0 / perc pno / viola bass.
Commissioned by the Serge Koussevitzky Music Foundation.
Composed: June 1983, New York City.
Publication: Novello, 89 0149, 1988, now available from Theodore Presser Company.
Premiere: Chatham College, Pittsburgh, Pennsylvania, October 22, 1984; The Pittsburgh New Music Ensemble conducted by David Stock.

Manuscript: The printed score is a reproduction of the composer's manuscript. A copy of the score is in the Library of Congress, Bazelon Collection, box 31, 64 pp.

IB86. Quintessentials
For Flute, Clarinet, Marimba, Percussion and Bass
Commissioned by the New York Quintet.

Composed: August 1983, New York City.

Publication: Theodore Presser Company: rental.

Premiere: Percussive Arts Society Convention, Knoxville, Tennessee, November 4, 1983; New York Quintet.

Manuscript: Unknown. A copy of the work reproduced from the composer's manuscript is in the Library of Congress, Bazelon Collection, box 19, 20 pp.

IB87. Fourscore
For Percussion Quartet
Commissioned by the University of Wisconsin Music Department.

Composed: (1985). The date of composition is known from the date of the first performance.

Publication: Theodore Presser Company, 114 - 40584, 1991.

Premiere: Abbott Concert Hall, University of Wisconsin, River Falls, Wisconsin, May 7, 1985; Heather Barringer, Lisa Benz, David Niebuhr, Peter O'Gorman, percussion; conducted by J. Michael Roy.

Manuscript: Library of Congress, Bazelon Collection, box 10, ink on transparencies, 12 pp.

IB88. Trajectories
For Piano with Orchestra
For: picc 2 2 bclt 2 cfg / 4 3 3 1 / timp 5perc / strings.

Written for Wanda Maximilien.

Composed: September 1985, New York City.

Publication: Theodore Presser Company, 416 - 41128, 1992.

Premiere: Not yet publicly performed, recorded in 1992 on Albany Records CD Troy 054 by Wanda Maximilien and the London Philharmonic Orchestra conducted by Harold Farberman.

Manuscript: The printed score is a reproduction of the composer's manuscript. The original is in the Library of Congress, Bazelon Collection, box 10, pencil on manuscript paper, 130 pp.

IB89. Symphony No. 8
For Strings

Commissioned by and dedicated to Harold Farberman and the Conductor's Institute. Also dedicated to Richard Rodney Bennett on his 50th birthday.

Composed: April 1986, New York City.

Publication: Theodore Presser Company, 416 - 41124, 1991.

Premiere: Koger Auditorium, University of South Carolina, Columbia, South Carolina, July 6, 1990; Institute Orchestra conducted by Harold Farberman.

Manuscript: Unknown. The printed score is a reproduction of the composer's manuscript. A copy of the printed score is in the Library of Congress, Bazelon Collection, box 32, 86 pp.

IB90. Motivations
For Solo Trombone and Orchestra

For: picc 2 2 2 bclt 2 cfg / 4 3 2 1 / timp 3perc pno / strings.

Composed: August 1986, New York City.

Publication: Theodore Presser Company: rental.

Premiere: Not yet performed.

Manuscript: Unknown. A copy of the work which is a reproduction of the composer's manuscript is in the Library of Congress, Bazelon Collection, box 19, 41 pp.

IB91. Legends and Love Letters
Five Songs from Hart Crane Poems
For Soprano and Chamber Ensemble

For: 1 (:alt & picc) 0 1 (:bclt) 0 / 0 0 0 0 / perc pno / vla vc.
Dedicated to Joan Heller and Collage.

> 1: My Grandmother's Love Letters
> 2: March
> 3: Legend
> 4: Forgetfulness
> 5: October - November
> Hart Crane (1899 - 1932)

Composed: April - May 1987, New York City.

Publication: Theodore Presser Company, 411 - 41094, 1991.

Premiere: Hirshhorn Museum Auditorium, Smithsonian Institute, Washington, D.C., November 5, 1988; Joan Heller, soprano; Collage New Music Chamber Ensemble conducted by Christopher Kendall.

Manuscript: Unknown. The printed score is a reproduction of the composer's manuscript. A copy of the score is in the Library of Congress, Bazelon Collection, box 31, 56 pp. The manuscript of a sixth song, a setting of "Old Song," not used in the cycle, is in the Library of Congress, Bazelon Collection, box 11, pencil and crayon on manuscript paper, 3 pp.

IB92. Fourscore + 2
For Percussion Quartet and Orchestra
For: picc 2 2 Ehn 2 bclt 2 cfg / 4 3 3 1 / timp pno / strings.
Some movements of this work are identical to IB87.
Composed: June - September 1987, Watermill, New York.
Publication: Theodore Presser Company: rental.
Premiere: Shepherd School of Music, Rice University, Houston, Texas,
     April 26, 1989; Continuum Percussion Quartet; Shepherd School
     Symphony Orchestra conducted by Gisèle Ben-Dor.
Manuscript: Unknown. A copy of the work reproduced from the
     composer's manuscript is in the Library of Congress, Bazelon
     Collection, box 19, 80 pp.

IB93. Symphony No. 8½
For Orchestra
For: picc 2 2 2 bclt 2 / 2 2 2 1 / timp 3perc pno / strings.
Composed: August 1988, New York City.
Publication: Theodore Presser Company, 416 - 41135, 1996.
Premiere: Carnegie Hall, New York City, May 11, 1997; American
     Composers Orchestra conducted by Paul Lustig Dunkel.
Manuscript: Library of Congress, Bazelon Collection, box 11, pencil on
     manuscript paper mounted on paper, 59 pp.

IB94. Fairy Tale
For Solo Viola and Chamber Ensemble
For: 1 (:picc) 0 1 bclt 0 / 1 1 0 0 / perc pno / vc bass.
Composed: May 1989, New York City.
Publication: Theodore Presser Company, 416 - 41132, 1993.
Premiere: Merkin Concert Hall, New York City, October 2, 1989; Lois
     Martin, viola; North-South Consonance conducted by the composer.
Manuscript: The printed score is a reproduction of the composer's
     manuscript. The original is in the Library of Congress, Bazelon
     Collection, box 12, pencil on manuscript paper, 53 pp.

IB95. Alliances
For Cello and Piano
Written for Dorothy Lawson and Faine Wright.
Composed: August 1989, Watermill, New York.
Publication: Theodore Presser Company, 114 - 40708, 1993.
Premiere: Weill Recital Hall, New York City, May 21, 1991; Dorothy
     Lawson, cello; Faine Wright, piano.
Manuscript: Library of Congress, Bazelon Collection, box 12, pencil on
     manuscript paper, 28 pp.

IB96. Sunday Silence
For Solo Piano
Commissioned by Alan Mandel.
Composed: November 1989, New York City.
Publication: Theodore Presser Company, 410 - 41295, 1993.
Premiere: Weill Recital Hall, New York City, October 1, 1990; Alan
   Mandel.
Manuscript: The printed score is a reproduction of the composer's
   manuscript. The original is in the Library of Congress, Bazelon
   Collection, box 12, pencil on paper mounted on paper, 15 pp.

IB97. Midnight Music
For Symphonic Wind Band
Commissioned by Timothy Reynish and the Royal Northern College
   Wind Band.
Composed: April 1990, New York City.
Publication: Novello, 1990.
Premiere: Royal Northern College of Music, Manchester, England,
   October 7, 1992; Royal Northern College Wind Band conducted by
   Timothy Reynish.
Manuscript: The printed score is a reproduction of the composer's
   manuscript. The original is in the Library of Congress, Bazelon
   Collection, box 13, pencil and ink on paper, 84 pp.

IB98. Prelude to Hart Crane's "The Bridge"
For String Ensemble
For: 6 6 4 4 3.
Commissioned by the Chicago String Ensemble.
Composed: May 1991, New York City.
Publication: Theodore Presser Company, 416 - 41133, 1994.
Premiere: St. Paul's Church, Chicago, Illinois, November 6, 1992;
   Chicago String Ensemble conducted by Alan Heatherington.
Manuscript: Library of Congress, Bazelon Collection, box 13, pencil on
   manuscript paper, 18 pp.

IB99. Four . . . Parts of a World
Song Cycle for Soprano and Piano
From Poems by Wallace Stevens
                    1: Girl in a Nightgown
                    2: On the Adequacy of Landscape
                    3: Dezembrum
                    4: The Candle a Saint
                              from Parts of a World,
                              Wallace Stevens (1879 - 1955)

Composed: August 1991, Sagaponack, New York.

Publication: Theodore Presser Company, 111 - 40135, 1993, 1994.

Premiere: Tsai Performance Center, Boston University, Boston, Massachusetts, November 4, 1992; Joan Heller, soprano; Thomas Stumpf, piano.

Manuscript: Library of Congress, Bazelon Collection, box 13, pencil on manuscript paper mounted on paper, 31 pp.

IB100. Bazz Ma Tazz
For Twelve Trombones and Six Percussion
For eight trombones, four bass trombones and six percussionists
Written for Frank Epstein.

Composed: March 1992, New York City.

Publication: Theodore Presser Company, 414 - 41175, 1998.

Premiere: Jordan Hall, New England Conservatory of Music, Boston, Massachusetts, April 26, 1993; New England Conservatory Percussion Ensemble conducted by Frank Epstein.

Manuscript: Library of Congress, Bazelon Collection, box 15, pencil on manuscript paper mounted on paper, 49 pp.

IB101. Symphony No. 9
(Sunday Silence)
For orchestra: picc 2 2 2 bcl 2 cfg / 4 3 3 1 / timp 4perc pno / strings.

Dedicated to Sunday Silence, winner of the 1989 Kentucky Derby and voted Horse of the Year.

Composed: May 1992, New York City.

Publication: Theodore Presser Company, 416 - 41143, 1996.

Premiere: Not yet publicly performed, recorded in 1995 on Albany Records CD Troy 174 by Scott Dunn, piano; Bournemouth Symphony Orchestra conducted by Harold Farberman.

Manuscript: The printed score is a reproduction of the composer's manuscript. The original is in the Library of Congress, Bazelon Collection, box 14, pencil on paper, 40 pp.

IB102. Entre Nous
For Cello and Orchestra
For: picc 2 2 2 bcl 2 / 2 2 2 1 / timp 4perc / strings.

Written for Dorothy Lawson.

Composed: November 1992, New York City.

Publication: Theodore Presser Company, 416 - 41142, 1997.

Premiere: Washington Irving High School, New York City, February 6, 1994; Dorothy Lawson, cello; Greenwich Village Symphony Orchestra conducted by Robert Grehan.

Manuscript: Library of Congress, Bazelon Collection, box 14, pencil on manuscript paper partly mounted on paper, 61 pp.

IB103. Fire and Smoke

For Timpani and Symphonic Wind Band

Written for Jonathan Haas and the Aspen Music Festival Wind Ensemble.

Composed: May 1994, New York City.

Publication: Theodore Presser Company, 416 - 41145, 1997.

The reference to *Compulsion* by Irwin Bazelon that occurs on the final page of the score is an error for *Propulsions*.

Premiere: Bayer-Benedict Music Tent, Aspen, Colorado, July 4, 1994; Jonathan Hass, timpani; Aspen Music Festival Band conducted by Peter Jaffe.

Manuscript: Library of Congress, Bazelon Collection, box 15, pencil on paper mounted on paper, 29 pp.

IB104. The Bridge

For narrator and orchestra to a poem by Hart Crane. Three unfinished fragments of the work sketched in short scores. They include references to woodwind, brass, percussion and strings and specifically to oboe, clarinet, three trumpets, marimba, vibraphone, chimes, timpani and solo piano. A formal outline indicates that Bazelon was intending that **Prelude to Hart Crane's "The Bridge,"** IB98, for strings, would be the first movement. The most substantial fragment is five pages of short score giving the opening of the second movement, a setting of the first four stanzas of *Proem: To Brooklyn Bridge,* for narrator and orchestra. The second fragment is a one-page sketch of the opening of the third movement, a setting of *Ave Maria* for solo narrator. The fourth movement was to have been a choral setting of *Powhatan's Daughter.* The third fragment may be the opening of a fifth movement for orchestra. The words "solo piano" have been added between the fifth and sixth movements with an indication that a setting of *The Tunnel* was being contemplated. The sixth movement would have been a setting of *Atlantis* for soprano. Another formal outline, with more detailed comments, suggests that Bazelon also contemplated writing a work in eight parts, one for each of the poems that comprise Hart Crane's *The Bridge,* with an introductory setting of *Proem: To Brooklyn Bridge.*

Composed: 1995.

Publication: Unpublished.

Manuscript: Composer's Estate, pencil on manuscript paper. A photocopy of the unfinished score is in the Library of Congress,

Bazelon Collection, box 15, 5 incomplete pages plus 3 pages of rough sketches.

Other Works

(1) Arrangements

In Dulci Jubilo
Arranged for SATB chorus, 1955. See IB43.
Selections from the English and French Suites by J. S. Bach
Arranged and transcribed for string orchestra, November 1945.
Bound by the Kayser Music Binding Company, Chicago.
Library of Congress, Bazelon Collection, box J, ink on manuscript
paper, 25 pp.
Symphonic Etudes (Schumann Op. 13)
Orchestrated for 3 2 2 2 / 4 3 3 1 / timp perc hrp / strings,
February 1945.
Bound by the Kayser Music Binding Company, Chicago.
Library of Congress, Bazelon Collection, box J, ink on manuscript
paper, 116 pp.

(2) Commercials

AC Oil Filter, Robert Lawrence Productions.
no score, film reel only.
Library of Congress, Bazelon Collection, box R.
AC Spark Plugs
short score and parts.
Library of Congress, Bazelon Collection, box 24.
Alka Seltzer
full score and parts.

Library of Congress, Bazelon Collection, box 24.
American Cyanamide Company (for Cunningham and Walsh).
1: Aureomycin, 1963.
> short score and parts.
> Library of Congress, Bazelon Collection, box 24.
2: Farm Journal, 1963.
> short score and parts.
> Library of Congress, Bazelon Collection, box 24.
Ban, Paul Kim.
> no score, film reel only.
> Library of Congress, Bazelon Collection, box R.
Ban-Bristol Myers
> full score and parts.
> Library of Congress, Bazelon Collection, box 24.
Best Foods, opening for TV "Riverboat."
> full score and parts.
> Library of Congress, Bazelon Collection, box 24.
Bryant Gas Air Conditioner
> no score, recording only.
> Library of Congress, Bazelon Collection, box R.
Bufferin
> no score, recording only.
> Library of Congress, Bazelon Collection, box R.
Buitoni
1: Handful
> short score and parts.
> Library of Congress, Bazelon Collection, box 24.
2: Tomato Plant
> short score and parts.
> Library of Congress, Bazelon Collection, box 24.
Burner with a Brain, Consolidated Gas.
> short score and parts.
> Library of Congress, Bazelon Collection, box 24.
Chesterfield
1: #1
> short score and parts.
> Library of Congress, Bazelon Collection, box 24.
2: Christmas Commercial
> short score and parts.
> Library of Congress, Bazelon Collection, box 24.
Chung-King
> short score and parts.
> Library of Congress, Bazelon Collection, box 24.
Colban

short score and parts.

Library of Congress, Bazelon Collection, box 24.

Consolidated Gas Company, Chadwick.

no score, film reel only.

Library of Congress, Bazelon Collection, box R.

Cut-Rite Wax Paper

no score, recording only.

Library of Congress, Bazelon Collection, box R.

Encyclopedia Britannica, Traveler Wanted, McCann-Erikson, 1965.

short score and parts.

Library of Congress, Bazelon Collection, box 24.

Esquire Lano Way

negative score and parts.

Library of Congress, Bazelon Collection, box 24.

Esso, news and weather theme.

no score, film reel only.

Library of Congress, Bazelon Collection, box R.

GE Billboard, opening music.

short score.

Library of Congress, Bazelon Collection, box 24.

Gift Star

parts.

Library of Congress, Bazelon Collection, box 24.

Gillette "Helpful Suggestions"

short score and parts.

Library of Congress, Bazelon Collection, box 24.

Hamilton Electric Watch

short score and parts.

Library of Congress, Bazelon Collection, box 25.

Hélène Curtis

short score and parts.

Library of Congress, Bazelon Collection, box 25.

Ipana

1: Little Mother, 1953.

short score and parts.

Library of Congress, Bazelon Collection, box 25.

2: Cowboys

short score and parts.

Library of Congress, Bazelon Collection, box 25.

Kellogg's Big K Family, August 1974.

short score and parts.

Library of Congress, Bazelon Collection, box 25.

Knickerbocker Beer, Robert Lawrence Productions.

no score, film reel only.
Library of Congress, Bazelon Collection, box R.

Kool

short score and parts.
Library of Congress, Bazelon Collection, box 25.

Molson's Brewery, Sarra Productions.

no score, film reel only.
Library of Congress, Bazelon Collection, box R.

Nabisco "Chippers"

short score and parts.
Library of Congress, Bazelon Collection, box 25.

National Insurance

no score, recording only.
Library of Congress, Bazelon Collection, box R.

Nestea

no score, recording only.
Library of Congress, Bazelon Collection, box R.

New Steels, October 1966.

no score, recording only.
Library of Congress, Bazelon Collection, box R.

Noxzema

1: Summer Beauty, February 5, 1958.

short score and parts.
Library of Congress, Bazelon Collection, box 25.

2: Three Windows

short score and parts.
Library of Congress, Bazelon Collection, box 25.

3: #3, Elektra Films for J.W. Thomson.

no score, recording only.
Library of Congress, Bazelon Collection, box R.

Old Stoker, train music for unidentified commercial.

no score, recording only.
Library of Congress, Bazelon Collection, box R.

Prudential

short score and parts.
Library of Congress, Bazelon Collection, box 25.

RCA Victor Records

short score and parts.
Library of Congress, Bazelon Collection, box 25.

Samsonite Luggage

short score and parts.
Library of Congress, Bazelon Collection, box 25.

Sanforised, Lars Calonius.

no score, film reel only.

Library of Congress, Bazelon Collection, box R.
Sanka Coffee, Audio Productions.
  no score, film reel only.
  Library of Congress, Bazelon Collection, box R.
Sanka Cut-outs
  full score and parts.
  Library of Congress, Bazelon Collection, box 25.
Spree
  no score, recording only.
  Library of Congress, Bazelon Collection, box R.
Standard Oil of New Jersey, Esso
  no score, film reel only.
  Library of Congress, Bazelon Collection, box R.
Sturbridge Village: Early America, Sherwin Williams Paint.
  short score and parts.
  Library of Congress, Bazelon Collection, box 25.
Timken Roller Bearings
  full score and parts.
  Library of Congress, Bazelon Collection, box 25.
Tip-Top Bread
  no score, recording only.
  Library of Congress, Bazelon Collection, box R.
Tip-Top Conversions
  short score and parts.
  Library of Congress, Bazelon Collection, box 25.
Union Carbide
  short score and parts.
  Library of Congress, Bazelon Collection, box 25.

Note: The source given for each work in the above list is the primary source, that is the manuscript score of the work, where it exists, rather than a recording of it. The original recordings of these works are also in the Library of Congress, Bazelon Collection.

(3) Films, Documentaries and Industrials

Africa, Poverty Films, June 25, 1968.
  Introduction (40 seconds).
  short score and parts.
  Library of Congress, Bazelon Collection, box 20.
American Petroleum Institute, film by Pendulum Productions, May 18, 1964.
  full score and parts.
  Library of Congress, Bazelon Collection, box 22.

American Telephone and Telegraph
1: Big City Finale, Fred Niles, March 11, 1963.
    short score and parts.
    Library of Congress, Bazelon Collection, box 22.
2: The Information Explosion, February 8, 1963.
    short score and parts.
    Library of Congress, Bazelon Collection, box 22.
3: The Vital Link, March 4, 1963.
    short score and parts.
    Library of Congress, Bazelon Collection, box 22.
The Answer Machine
    short score and parts.
    Library of Congress, Bazelon Collection, box 22.
Breck, in-house film, March 10, 1965.
    short score and parts.
    Library of Congress, Bazelon Collection, box 22.
Building America, Pintoff, a public service film.
    short score and parts.
    Library of Congress, Bazelon Collection, box 22.
Catholic Charities, documentary, March 8, 1968.
    short score and parts.
    Library of Congress, Bazelon Collection, box 20.
Cedarbrook Hill, short film, December 20, 1963.
    short score and parts.
    Library of Congress, Bazelon Collection, box 20.
Corbett House, documentary for Willard Van Dyke, June 2 1965.
    short score and parts.
    Library of Congress, Bazelon Collection, box 20.
    Material later used in **Early American Suite,** IB55.
Elizabeth Taylor in London, Pelican Films.
    no score, film reel only.
    Library of Congress, Bazelon Collection, box R.
Esso for McCann Erickson. Two short films.
    short scores and parts.
    Library of Congress, Bazelon Collection, box 22.
Eye in Space, industrial film for IBM.
    short score and parts.
    Library of Congress, Bazelon Collection, box 20.
Food for Peace, Willard Van Dyke, January 21, 1963.
    no score, recording only.
    Library of Congress, Bazelon Collection, box R.
The Girl Game, Milton Greene and Joe Eula Productions, July 19, 1967.
    short score and parts.
    Library of Congress, Bazelon Collection, box 20.

Girl-Scouts of America, film, January 1951.

> The music for the film can be found in a version called **The Growing Years, Suite for Small Orchestra.**
> Library of Congress, Bazelon Collection, box 29.
> Published in 1956 as **Suite for Small Orchestra,** IB38.

Gold, the Sacred Metal, Rena productions, documentary.

> full score and parts.
> Library of Congress, Bazelon Collection, box 20.

Greyhound Bus

> full score and parts.
> Library of Congress, Bazelon Collection, box 23.

History of Gas Stations, industrial film for Texaco by Skyline Productions, August 1964.

> no score, recording only.
> Library of Congress, Bazelon Collection, box R.

The Hope that Jack Built, documentary for the National Association of Investment Companies, Robert Lawrence.

> full score and parts.
> Library of Congress, Bazelon Collection, box 20.

The Human Element, documentary by Searchinger and Boyd for Pendulum Productions, June 1963.

> No score or recording extant.

Inquiry, IBM Air Force film, Henry Strauss Productions.

> short score.
> Library of Congress, Bazelon Collection, box R.

The Ivory Knife, art film by Jules Engel for Martha Jackson Gallery on the painter Paul Jenkins, August 26, 1965.

> short score and parts.
> Library of Congress, Bazelon Collection, box 27.
> The film is in the film archive of the Museum of Modern Art, New York.

J.Manorville, Skyline Films.

> short score and parts.
> Library of Congress, Bazelon Collection, box 23.

Laser Lights and Atoms, documentary, November 1968.

> short score and parts.
> Library of Congress, Bazelon Collection, box 21.

Lennox Glass

> no score, film reel only.
> Library of Congress, Bazelon Collection, box R.

National Guard

> short score and parts.
> Library of Congress, Bazelon Collection, box 23.

New York 100, art film by Jules Engel for the Martha Jackson Gallery on the painter John Hultberg, including the three minute segment "Walking Through the City" and another "Probing the Psyche," March 27, 1967.
short score and parts, score only of "Walking Through the City" and "Probing the Psyche."
Library of Congress, Bazelon Collection, box 27.

Of Earth and Fire, documentary by Ralph Steiner and Wheaton Galantine, October 13, 1967.
short score and parts.
Library of Congress, Bazelon Collection, box 21.

Overture to Tomorrow, documentary by Skyline Films for Hewitt Robbins, 1966. The music was recorded first and then the film was shot without narration.
short score and parts.
Library of Congress, Bazelon Collection, box 21.
Material later used in **Symphony no. 5,** IB57.

The Pond and The City, Knickerbocker Films.
short score and parts.
Library of Congress, Bazelon Collection, box 21.

Research Institute, American Slide Films.
no score, recording only.
Library of Congress, Bazelon Collection, box R.

Rice, Willard Van Dyke documentary for Rockefeller Foundation.
short score and parts, also printed catalogue.
Library of Congress, Bazelon Collection, box 21.

Saudi Arabia, documentary, Ray Graham Associates.
no score, recording only.
Library of Congress, Bazelon Collection, box R.

School House, Lowry Productions for Pelican Film, 1963.
short score and parts.
Library of Congress, Bazelon Collection, box 23.

Scope, Skyline Films for Hewitt Robbins, March 1967.
parts only.
Library of Congress, Bazelon Collection, box 23.

Standard Oil, Lowry Productions, Pendulum Films, December 14, 1962.
no score, film reel only.
Library of Congress, Bazelon Collection, box R.

Suffer the Little Children, documentary for the Lutheran Church by Vision Associates.
short score and parts.
Library of Congress, Bazelon Collection, box 21.

Texaco, two short films for Skyline Productions, August 14, 1963.
short scores and parts.

Library of Congress, Bazelon Collection, box 23.

Note: The source given for each work in the above list is the primary source, that is the manuscript score of the work, where it exists, rather than a recording of it. The original recordings of these works are also in the Library of Congress, Bazelon Collection.

(4) Incidental Music for Theatrical Productions

Incidental Music for *Liliom*. A play in seven scenes and a prologue by F. Molnar. Scored for flute, clarinet, bassoon and trumpet. Score dated May 3, 1949, New York City.
Library of Congress, Bazelon Collection, box 29, 17 pp.

Incidental Music to John Huston's *Frankie and Johnny* produced by the De Lys Theater Corporation at Theater de Lys, New York, September 29 - October 25, 1952.
Score no longer extant. No recording of the music.

Incidental Music to Shakespeare's *The Merry Wives of Windsor*. Composed for the American Shakespeare Festival Theater, Stratford, Connecticut, production directed by John Houseman, 1959. Scored for 1 0 1 1/ 1 2 0 1 / perc.
Library of Congress, Bazelon Collection, box 29.
In 1960 material from the score was arranged to form the **Suite from Shakespeare's "The Merry Wives of Windsor,"** IB45.

Incidental Music to Shakespeare's *The Taming of the Shrew*. Composed for the American Shakespeare Festival Theater, Stratford, Connecticut, production directed by John Houseman, 1958.
Library of Congress, Bazelon Collection, box 29.
In 1960 the Overture was revised to become an independent work, **Overture to Shakespeare's "The Taming of the Shrew,"** IB46.

Three Abstractions (Ballet-Suite) for flute, saxophone (bass clarinet), bassoon, trumpet, piano and optional piano, 1948. See IB29.

Winter Wake. Ballet solo for piano, dancer and voice narration, 1949. See IB33.

(5) Library Music for Boosey and Hawkes written under the pseudonym Budd Graham.

Bazelon created the pseudonym by adding a "d" to "Bud" and using the middle name of his brother Edward, "Graham."
Most of the music written under this pseudonym was composed in 1966.
Library of Congress, Bazelon Collection, box 30.

Three Pieces for Ten Musicians
      (1) **Parade of the Taxi Cabs**, 12 pp.
      (2) **Slow March for a Robot**, 11 pp.
      (3) **Clem's Capers**, 3 pp.
Pieces for Ensemble
      A Day at the Circus, 7 pp.
      Ballet "Baby Chimpanzee," 1 p.
      Beyond the Stars, 4 pp.
      Dance for Two Chickens and Seven Eggs, 1 p.
      Follow the Leader, 7 pp.
      Probing the Psyche, 1 p.
            Also used in **New York 100**.
      Restless Colors in a Quiet Frame, 10 pp.
            The theme of this work was used as the basis for **A Quiet Piece ... for a violent time, IB65.**
      Walking Through the City, 5 pp.
Piano Collage
      Dance, 2 pp.
      Desolation (Aftermath of a Holocaust), 1 p.
      Duet for Two Calves, 1 p.
      Fugue for Cadillac, Ford and Two Volkswagens, 1 p.
      Hopscotch, 1 p.
      Lonely Lament, 1 p.
      Old Smokey (train), 3 pp.
      Out of the Tunnel, On to the Highway, 4 pp.
      Questions and Answers, 1 p.
      Seaside Frolic, 2 pp.
      Slum Sequence, 2 pp.
      Solitude, 1 p.
      Telephone and Telegraph Network, 1 p.
      Traffic Tie-up, 2 pp.
Pieces on tape for which the original score is no longer extant:
      A Day at the Circus
      Ball Games
      Dirge ... "In the Morgue"
      Fanfare for Skyscrapers
      Lazy Summer Afternoons
      Merry-Go-Rounds
      On the Launching Pad ... An "Eye" to Space
      Petulance
      Playground Romp
      "Reflections" ... Quiet Interlude
      Swings and Seesaws
      Teeter-Totters and Swings

Pieces on record for which the original score is no longer extant:
    The Animated Scarecrow
    Country Hay-Ride
    Dance for a Tomboy
        based on a movement from the **Suite for Young People,**
        IB37B.
    Little Miss-Summer's Night Dream
    Lyric Piece
    Pastoral
    Propellers and Open Cockpits
    Sleight of Hand
    Volcanic Events
    3½ Men on a Horse

(6) Television and Movies

Armstrong Circle Theater Opening, CBS TV.
    short score and parts.
    Library of Congress, Bazelon Collection, box 26.
Danny Kaye Opening Music, (Juggler on a Trampoline) CBS.
    August 1963.
    short score and parts.
    Library of Congress, Bazelon Collection, box 26.
Depth Study, CBS TV film.
    short score and parts.
    Library of Congress, Bazelon Collection, box 26.
The Glory Of Their Times, TV special on the history of baseball by
    Bud Greenspan for Cappy Productions, January 31, 1969.
    short score and parts.
    Library of Congress, Bazelon Collection, box 26.
NBC News and Public Service Program Closing Theme, 1963.
    full score and parts.
    Library of Congress, Bazelon Collection, box 26.
Olympic Countdown, TV special by Bud Greenspan for Cappy
    Productions, September 26, 1979.
    full score and parts.
    Library of Congress, Bazelon Collection, box 26.
Sale of the Century, Jones-Howard Productions, September 1969.
    no score, recording only.
    Library of Congress, Bazelon Collection, box R.
Science All Stars, Honeywell, ABC-TV.
1: Opening "Space" Theme
2: Billboard Opening
    short scores and parts.

Library of Congress, Bazelon Collection, box 27.

Survival 67, full length feature-documentary on the Six-Day War, written by Irwin Shaw, directed by Jules Dassin, 1968.

incomplete score, complete parts.

Library of Congress, Bazelon Collection, box 28.

Material later used in **Symphony No. 6,** IB59.

Thirty-Six Maiden Lane, TV pilot for Jerome Hellman.

Main titles (Dirge on the Hill) and other material.

Incomplete score, some cues on demo tracks.

Library of Congress, Bazelon Collection, box 27.

TV Investigators

No score, theme on various demo tracks.

Library of Congress, Bazelon Collection, box R.

What Makes Sammy Run? Two hour TV special from Budd Schulberg novel, NBC TV, December 1959.

score and parts.

Library of Congress, Bazelon Collection, box 27.

Wilma, full-length TV movie on Olympic runner Wilma Rudolph by Bud Greenspan for Cappy Productions, October 14, 1977. Scored for 1 1 1 1 / 2 2 2 0 / timp perc pno / strings.

full score and parts.

Library of Congress, Bazelon Collection, box 28.

Note: The source given for each work in this list is the primary source, that is the manuscript score of the work, where it exists, rather than a recording of it. The original recordings of these works are also in the Library of Congress, Bazelon Collection.

(7) Unidentified Pieces

Cab on the Street, 6 pp.

Library of Congress, Bazelon Collection, box 30.

Judy's Music for solo piano, 1 p.

Library of Congress, Bazelon Collection, box 30.

Various unidentified sketches.

Library of Congress, Bazelon Collection, box 30.

Note: The references to box R in the Library of Congress, Bazelon Collection are to a collection of recordings that are housed in boxes that have not, at the time of writing, been given a numerical designation.

Bazelon in Print

"**A Composer's Views**." *The New York Times,* May 8, 1949. Letter about the difficulties faced by composers, the writing of chamber music in order to obtain performances and the kinds of pieces that orchestras are willing to programme. The letter ends with an exhortation to serious composers to continue to write until conductors are more willing to programme contemporary music.

"**A Modest Proposal: Some Thoughts on the Pulitzer Prize**." *Collage New Music Newsletter,* 1988. Letter suggesting that the Pulitzer Prize Panel should award more than one prize a year and analysing the consequences of such a proposal.

"**An Open Letter to the Members of AMC**." *American Music Center Newsletter,* 1983. Letter describing how keeping a score of *De-Tonations* at the American Music Center led directly to performances in Carnegie Hall and by the National Orchestra of France (Lille).

"**An Immodest Proposal?**" *ASCAP Newsletter,* 1981. Letter suggesting that composers should be given the opportunity to commission the orchestra instead of the reverse.

"**Banjo Culture**." *The New York Post,* August 27, 1977. Letter about the death of Elvis Presley and the effect he had upon culture. [Bazelon received hate mail after the publication of the letter].

"**Cyrano de Bergerac**." *Film Music Notes,* January 1951, 8 pp. Review of Dimitri Tiomken's score for *Cyrano de Bergerac.*

"**From Irwin Bazelon, Composer**." *Mohawk Trail Concerts, 25th Anniversary Catalogue*, 1994. Item in which Bazelon recollects problems encountered in conducting a performance of *Sound Dreams* some years previously.

"**Knowing the Score: Notes on Film Music**." Van Nostrand Reinhold, 1975, 352 pp.

"**Knowing the Score: Notes on Film Music.**" Paperback edition by Arco Publishing, Inc., 1981, 352 pp.

"**The Heiress**." *Film Music Notes*, vol. ix, no. 2, Nov-Dec 1949, pp. 17-18. Review of Copland's score for *The Heiress*.

"**The Readers React to Rorem vs Goldstein**." *The New York Times*, November 16, 1969. Letter on the clash between popular culture and serious music arising from comments by Ned Rorem.

"**Thoughts on the Pulitzer Prize**." *ASCAP Newsletter*, 1989. Letter.

"**Woman with a Symphony**." Article on Marion Bauer, *The Baton* (DePaul University), vol. xxx, no. 3, 1951, pp. 4-7.

Bibliography

1   "Alliances." Chamber Music (Summer 1991).

News item about the world premiere of *Alliances*. Includes brief details about the performers and about the composer.

2   "American Composer Update." *Pan Pipes of Sigma Alpha Iota* (Winter, 1980).
Details of Bazelon's activities in 1979, premieres (*Imprints* and *De-Tonations*), other performances (*Double Crossings, Duo for Viola* (incorrectly stated as violin) *and Piano, Sound Dreams* and *Partnership*), publications (*Double Crossings, Propulsions* (Boosey and Hawkes), *Imprints, De-Tonations, Duo* (Novello)), recordings (*Woodwind Quintet*) and other news with details of lectures given by the composer.

3   "American Composer Update." *Pan Pipes of Sigma Alpha Iota* (Winter 1981).
Details of Bazelon's activities in 1980, premieres (*Three Men on a Dis-Course, Partnership*), other performances (anticipating *De-Tonations* by the L'Orchestre National de France in 1981), publications (three Novello works given in 2 and *Partnership*).

4   "American Composer Update." *Pan Pipes of Sigma Alpha Iota* (Winter 1983).
See 129.

5   "American Composer Update." *Pan Pipes of Sigma Alpha Iota* (Winter
         1992).
         Details of Bazelon's activities in 1991, premieres (*Alliances*), other
         performances (*Midnight Music*), publications (*Symphony No. 8, Legends
         and Love Letters, Fourscore* (Theodore Presser)), recordings
         (*Trajectories, Spires, Legends and Love Letters*), and other news
         anticipating future performances.

6   "Angry Composer." *Newsweek* (December 17, 1962).
         Article describing Bazelon's reaction to the world premiere of his *Short
         Symphony, Testimonial to a Big City* by the National Symphony
         Orchestra in Washington. The symphony is described as bristling "with
         the noisy restless tensions and explosive undercurrents of a big city." In a
         discussion of the problems encountered by professional composers in
         making a living, Bazelon calls for more financial support for creative
         artists. He comments on how he has supported himself "by playing the
         horses" and by foundation grants but "largely by composing background
         music for industrial documentaries." He describes his commercial music
         as "exactly the same" as "I write for concerts," remarking that he is not
         "schizophrenic" about his music.

7   "The Ballad of Big Bud." *Time Magazine* (May 20, 1966).
         Article about Bazelon's love of horse racing and its effect on his work as
         a composer. The inspiration of the racetrack as "an extension of the pulse
         and rhythmic beat of the city" is noted and the finale of *Dramatic
         Movement for Orchestra* is described as his version of "horses thundering
         down the stretch at the Aqueduct." Describes how winnings at Aqueduct
         in 1958 provided the funds to record the *Concert Ballet.* This led to the
         premiere of the *Short Symphony,* just recorded by the Louisville
         Orchestra. Anticipates the composition of the *Churchill Downs Concerto*
         in response to the experience of seeing his first Kentucky Derby. Also
         refers to his composition studies at DePaul University in Chicago, then
         with Hindemith at Yale and finally with Milhaud at Mills College in
         California. Describes his settling in New York in 1948 and working as a
         railroad reservations clerk while attempting to become established as a
         composer. Discusses the curing of his childhood deafness after which
         "the violent, silent world inside" him "suddenly erupted." References to
         compositional activities include writing music for commercials (Ipana,
         Buitoni, Noxzema) and the NBC-TV news theme. Bazelon describes
         himself as the "father of contemporary music in commercials" and notes
         that he writes the "same kind of music for toothpaste and spaghetti" as he
         does "for the concert hall." Includes a photograph of Bazelon and his
         wife at the Kentucky Derby with a subtitle that continues the racing
         theme: "His kingdom for a horse."

8   "Bazelon to Conduct Symphony Tuesday." *The Washington Sunday Star*
        (December 12, 1962).
        Article anticipating the world premiere of the *Short Symphony,
        Testimonial to a Big City*. Describes Bazelon's interest in horse racing
        and his use of his Aqueduct Racetrack winnings to record examples of
        his music that led directly to the conductor of the National Symphony
        Orchestra, Howard Mitchell, deciding to perform the symphony. The
        potential audience reaction to the work is anticipated in a number of
        comments by the composer including his desire to avoid the typical
        "polite indifference" of American audiences and "my music is not urbane
        but it is urban" as it reflects his experience of city life in Chicago and
        New York. Bazelon also remarks that "a composer spends his life writing
        one long work which is broken off into segments which become
        symphonies, tone poems and other shorter works." Includes a
        photograph.

9   "Bazelon's World Premiere Here."   *The Seattle Post Intelligencer*
        (February 17, 1966).
        News item anticipating the world premiere of *Dramatic Movement for
        Orchestra*. Includes an account of how the conductor, Milton Katims,
        discovered the score. Brief biographical details of the composer include
        his studying with Milhaud and Bloch. Quotes Bazelon as stating that
        "there is in my music the relentless supercharged surge of city life that
        reflects the fact that I have lived all of my years in the city".

10   "Bettis Company Offers Premiere." *The New York Times* (August 19,
        1949).
        Review by J.M. of the first performance of *Three Abstractions (Ballet-
        Suite)*. States that the work is currently titled *It is Always Farewell* and
        that it is unfinished, only two movements being performed. Assesses the
        contribution of Bazelon's music to the overall introspective mood of the
        work.

11   "Birthday Music." *The New York Times* (April 6, 1973).
        News item anticipating the first New York performance of *Overture to
        Shakespeare's "The Taming of the Shrew"* in a concert celebrating the
        68th birthday of the Greenwich Music School.

12   "Blossom Fanfare Pieces Picked." *Cleveland Plain Dealer* (August 17,
        1970).
        News report about the Blossom Music Center fanfare competition. Gives
        brief details about the two winners, Bazelon and Walter Aschaffenbury.
        Notes that there were more than 200 entries and the competition was
        judged by Louis Lane and Donald Erb.

13   "Chamber Ensemble." *The New York Times* (January 21, 1957).
        Review by E.D. of the first public performance of *Sound Track for Seven
        Piece Set*. The reviewer criticised the title (which was later changed to
        Chamber Concerto No. 1) but praised the work for its rhythmic vitality
        and use of tone colour.

14   "Collage." *The Christian Science Monitor* (November 18, 1977).
        Review of the world premiere of *Sound Dreams*. The reviewer admired
        the setting up of "a basic netherworld - rather more intellectual and dry
        then picturesque."

15   "Composer Irwin Bazelon visits UW-River Falls." *River Falls Journal*
        (May 2, 1985).
        Article anticipating Bazelon's presence as commissioned-composer in
        residence at UW-River Falls and the world premiere of *Fourscore*. A
        brief review of the importance of percussion in Bazelon's music
        discusses the scoring of *Propulsions, Double Crossings, Triple Play* and
        Cross-Currents. Also anticipates a forthcoming performance of the
        Woodwind Quintet.

16   "Composers." *Musical America* (November 1963).
        Notes the world premiere of the *Symphony in One Movement* (No. 1).

17   "Composers and Performers." *American Musical Digest* (October 1969).
        Includes two reviews of the world premiere of *Symphony No. 5*, one by
        Charles Staff abridged from the Indianapolis News (249), the other by
        Corbin Patrick abridged from the Indianapolis Star (213). Includes a
        photograph.

18   "Composer's Concert Offers 3 New Works." *The New York Times*
        (February 9, 1948).
        Review by C.H. of the New York premiere (now the first known
        performance) of *Sonata No. 1 for Piano* (then just titled *Piano Sonata*).
        Offers no specific comments on Bazelon's work referring instead to
        general issues about the whole program such as the difficulty of
        understanding new music and its lack of melodic invention. Includes
        favourable comments on the performance of the pianist Bernardo Segall.

19   "Composer's Forum Gives First Concert of Season." *The New York
        Herald Tribune* (October 25, 1948).
        Review by A.V.B. of the world premieres of *Suite for Clarinet, Cello and
        Piano* and *String Quartet No. 2*. Describes the composer as "the all-too-
        familiar problem-child of the evening" noting that he "stems musically
        from the Viennese atonalists, but he is so unaware of, or indifferent to,

his origins that their indispensable expressivity and logic completely escape him."

20 "Composer's Forum Opens at Columbia." *The New York Times* (October 25, 1948).
Review by C.H. of the world premieres of *Suite for Clarinet, Cello and Piano* and *String Quartet No. 2.* Described as "complicated music" that "went so far out of its way to avoid melody or even sonority that it was impossible to grasp," adding that "one could only admire the energy which carried the composer along in such a dry idiom."

21 "Composer's League." *New York Herald Tribune* (February 9, 1948).
Review by A.V.B. of the world premiere of *Sonata No. 1 for Piano.* Described as "a student-piece of the 'wrong-note' school" and "completely lacking in aural sense."

22 "Le compositeur américain Irwin Bazelon dirigera le Philharmonique de Lille." *La Voix du Nord* (February 11, 1981).
News item about a performance of *De-Tonations.* Gives brief biographical details about the composer including the fact that he studied with Milhaud. Includes a photograph.

23 "Concert and Recital." *The New York Herald Tribune* (April 2, 1951).
Review by A.B. of the world premiere of *Five Pieces for Piano* by Ruth Strassman Bazelon. Notes that "Bazelon's music still needs more shape," but the "pieces had their moments."

24 "CRI SD287." *Brodart Listening Post* (May 1974).
Review of reissue of CRI SD287 (*Symphony No. 5, Churchill Downs*). Describes Bazelon as "displaying an amazing range of musical ability" noting various compositional activities including NBC-TV's *What Makes Sammy Run?* and Jules Dassin's *Survival 1967.*

25 "CRI SD287." *Consumer Reports* (January 2, 1973).
Review of reissue of CRI SD287 (*Symphony No. 5, Churchill Downs*). Describes *Symphony No. 5* as "intense and passionate" and a "tough and disturbing" work which "reveals Bazelon as a composer with much to say about our present condition." Includes brief biographical details.

26 "CRI SD287." *Fort Wayne News Sentinel* (June 2, 1972).
Brief review of CRI SD287 which includes *Symphony No. 5* and *Churchill Downs.* *Symphony No. 5* is described as "a tightly-knit and rewarding work" and the recording is "highly recommended."

27   "Cross-Currents." *The Patriot Ledger* (January 20, 1981).
        Review of the world premiere of *Cross-Currents*. Described as "an
        intriguing and often violent score" quoting the composer describing it as
        the "embodiment of the rebellious mutterings, cross-rhythms and nervous
        tension of the city."

28   "Elie Siegmeister." *Newsday* (January 17, 1989).
        Review of a performance of the *Sonatina for Piano* included in a concert
        designed to celebrate the 80th birthday of Elie Siegmeister. Notes that the
        work has "perpetually moving, motoric outer movements and a still,
        transparent middle movement."

29   "First Performances." *The World of Music* (UNESCO) (1970 no. 1).
        Gives details, in a list of first performances, of the world premiere of
        Symphony No. 5.

30   *"Frankie and Johnny* in Village Theater De Lys." *Caricature*
        (Greenwich Village's Feature Newspaper) (July 1952).
        Article about forthcoming production of *Frankie and Johnny* by John
        Huston with music by Irwin Bazelon. Includes a photograph of the
        composer, the first known example to appear in print.

31   "Hemidemisemiquavers." *The New York Times* (October 27, 1963).
        Brief news item noting the world premiere of *Symphony No. 1*.

32   "Honors for Alumni." *DePaul University Newsmagazine* (Winter 1972).
        Description of the Alumni Awards Convocation in which Bazelon was
        given an achievement award for outstanding accomplishment in his field.
        Notes Bazelon's various activities as a composer of orchestral music,
        film music and music for the American Shakespeare Festival Theater.
        Also includes comments by the composer in a composition class at the
        School of Music on the dedication and commitment required if
        composers are to find their "own sounds." Describing his own life "in the
        frenetic, nervous city," Bazelon used *Churchill Downs* and *Symphony
        No. 5* as examples to illustrate his music. Includes two photographs.

33   "Honors for Members." *ASCAP Today* (October 1969).
        Brief news report about the world premiere of *Symphony No. 5*. Includes
        a photograph.

34   "Honors for Members." *ASCAP Today* (March 1971).
        An entry noting the world premiere of *Symphony No. 6-Day War* and the
        Dramatic Fanfare for 1970 winning the fanfare competition sponsored
        by the Cleveland Orchestra and the Blossom Music Festival.

35   "Honors for Members." *ASCAP Today* (Winter 1975).
      An entry noting the world premiere of the *Woodwind Quintet*.

36   "Honors for Members." *ASCAP Today* (Fall 1976).
      Review of Bazelon's book *Knowing the Score: Notes on Film Music*.
      Observes that it includes "much information, some good interviews and
      helpful practical notes."

37   "The Hope that Jack Built." *Films for Business* (July 26, 1957).
      Review of the film *The Hope that Jack Built*. Describes Bazelon's
      original musical score as "unique and offbeat, worth hearing for its own
      sake. As counterpoint to the animation and scene switches it is extremely
      effective."

38   "How New York Critics See New Works by Living Composers." *Music
      News* (July 2, 1950).
      A synthesis of reviews of the world premiere of *Piano Sonata No. 2*
      taken from The New York Times (237) and the New York Herald
      Tribune (64).

39   "The Human Element." *The New York Times* (June 30, 1963).
      Review of the film *The Human Element,* made by Gene Searchinger and
      Scudder Boyd of Pendulum Productions with music by Irwin Bazelon.
      Includes brief but favourable comments on the music.

40   "Indianapolis Symphony To Record Bazelon Work." *The Indianapolis
      Herald* (November 30, 1971).
      As 81. The composer adds that *Churchill Downs* "does NOT describe
      the sights and sounds of the racetrack ... although it certainly has its pulse
      and beat."

41   "In Memoriam." *Yaddo News* (Fall 1996).
      Obituary. Notes that Bazelon had been a guest at Yaddo in 1969. Gives a
      brief account of his output, various performances, grants and
      commissions received. Also includes references to his activities as a
      lecturer, to his expertise on film music and his authorship of *Knowing the
      Score: Notes on Film Music*.

42   "Irwin Bazelon." *The East Hampton Star* (August 10, 1995).
      Obituary by S.S. Gives an account of Bazelon's life with references to
      "his first professional job as a composer and pianist for a Chicago dance
      band in the 1940s" and his composition studies with Hindemith and
      Milhaud. Notes he worked as a railroad reservations clerk before

becoming established as a professional composer writing for documentary films and commercials and the NBC-TV News theme. Also comments on his composing for productions of the American Shakespeare Theater, his authorship of *Knowing the* Score: *Notes on Film Music*, and his winning the Koussevitzky Prize in 1982 for his valuable contribution to contemporary music. Includes an account of how his favourite pastime, the racetrack, helped him launch his classical career, by using his winnings to record some of his music which led eventually to the premiere of his *Short Symphony*. Also notes the relationship between the racetrack and two compositions, *Churchill Downs* and *Sunday Silence*. Notes that he wrote nine symphonies and was working on a tenth, a large orchestral and choral piece based on the writings of Hart Crane, at the time of his death. Quotes comments by David Harold Cox taken from his article in the Bazelon brochure. Includes a photograph.

43   "Irwin Bazelon." *Percussive Notes* (Fall, 1979).
      Issue giving details of participants in the Percussive Arts Society International Convention, 1979. Lists Bazelon's most important works, his composition of incidental music for the American Shakespeare Festival Theater and for the NBC-TV production of *What Makes Sammy Run?* and *Wilma*, and his authorship of the book *Knowing the Score: Notes on Film Music*. Includes a photograph.

44   "Irwin Bazelon." *The Southampton Press* (August 10, 1995).
      Obituary. Describes Bazelon as "one of the most original and uncompromising modern composers." Brief details on Bazelon's early life include references to a "career as a jazz pianist in Chicago," the experience of hearing a performance of Beethoven's *Seventh Symphony* which changed his life, his musical studies at DePaul University then with Hindemith at Yale and Milhaud at Mills College. It describes his work as a professional composer in the 1950s and 60s before "creating orchestral music exclusively from the 1970s onward." States that he was composing his tenth symphony, an orchestral and choral piece based on the writings of Hart Crane, at the time of his death. Describes his music as being "known for a modern melodic structure that shifted between propulsive dynamic rhythms and extreme tenderness." Notes that Bazelon was "a horse racing enthusiast" and that he wrote "at least two pieces dedicated to the sport, *Churchill Downs* and *Sunday Silence*."

45   "Irwin Bazelon à Loos avec le Philharmonique." *La Voix du Nord* (February 18, 1981).
      Review of a performance of *De-Tonations* by the Lille Philharmonic Orchestra. The music is described as a rhythmic and emotional

experience and as "Des vagues se jetant sur les rochers, des gerbes sonores ou peut-être un feu d'artifice cuivré: quelque chose en dents de scie, juxtaposant l'inachevé, à la limite parfois de la dissonance." Notes that Bazelon was a pupil of Milhaud. Describes a variety of reactions from the audience to the work and acknowledges the contribution of the various organisations that made the concert possible. Includes a photograph.

46   "ISO To Feature Bazelon Symphony." *Indianapolis Star* (December 2, 1971).
Article announcing a performance of *Symphony No. 5* by the Indianapolis Orchestra prior to its recording for issue by Composers Recording Inc.

47   "The Ivory Knife." *Los Angeles Times* (July 10, 1966).
News item about *The Ivory Knife*, a film by Jules Engel with music by Irwin Bazelon, winning first prize in the painting and sculpture category at the Venice International Film Festival.

48   "Jonathan Haas Performs Rare Works on Timpani." *New York Times* (May 25, 1980).
Review of the world premiere of *Partnership for Timpani and Marimba*. Discusses the nature of the work in terms of the motivation of the composer creating an evocative mood rather than attempting to shock the listener.

49   "Klavierwunder aus Washington." *Else-Jetzel-Zeitung* (November 16, 1990).
Review of a performance of *Sunday Silence*. Notes that the work had just been premiered in Carnegie Hall and is dedicated to the memory of a famous racehorse. Described as "a wonderful study of motion and continuity."

50   "Korn Leads Last of Season's Bills." *The New York Times* (March 22, 1965).
Review by R.E. of the world premiere of *Concert Overture*. Notes that the work was written in 1952 and revised in 1960. Comments on the aggressive mood of the work, its scoring and its structure, and upon the individuality of its strong statements within current trends in contemporary music.

51   "Live Appearances." *Ovation* (Fall 1984).
Brief review of a performance of *Churchill Downs* as part of the Horizons 84 festival. The work is described as "rousing".

52   "Mohawk Trail Concerts welcomes three new artists at opener."
      Greenfield Recorder (July 4, 1996).
      News item anticipating a performance of *Alliances* by Dorothy Lawson
      and Scott Dunn in a concert of music by the "Four Big Bs: Bach,
      Beethoven, Brahms and Bazelon." Includes brief biographical details
      about the composer.

53   "Music Critics Hold 11th Annual Session, Enjoy Fine Concerts." *The
      Kansas City Star* (October 27, 1963).
      Account of the 4-day national meeting of The Music Critics Association
      in Kansas City. Notes that in the afternoon session a panel chaired by
      Thomas Sherman of the St. Louis Post-Dispatch and including Roger
      Sessions, Hans Schwieger and Irwin Bazelon, discussed the topic "What
      should the composers, critics, and conductors expect from each other?"

54   "Music in Our Time." *Musical America* (April 1964).
      Review by C.P.S. of the world premiere of the *Brass Quintet*. Notes that
      the work "is in a mid-ground chromatic style with a jazzy quality and
      several nice examples of fugues" but criticises the length of the piece.
      Comments favourably on the performance.

55   "Musique de notre temps." *Dernières Nouvelles D'Alsace* (March 13,
      1974).
      Review of a performance of the *Duo for Viola and Piano*. Remarks that
      "de carrure rhythmique plus traditionelle, le duo de Irwin Bazelon
      apportait une bienfaisante note concertante en guise d'épiloque."

56   "New Orleans Phil.: Bazelon Poem." *Musical America* (March 1976).
      Review by F.G. of the world premiere of *A Quiet Piece ... for a Violent
      Time*. Describes it as "a brooding work - an edgy meditation in the midst
      of holocaust." Quotes extensively from the programme notes for the
      concert. Comments on its "sparseness of musical means" and describes
      Bazelon as a "member of the minimalist school" but notes that he makes
      use of a "sustained musical line, achieved through lyricism and held
      tension."

57   "News and Honors." *ASCAP Today* (1975 no. 2).
      Notes the world premiere of the *Woodwind Quintet*.

58   "New Trends." *Tallahassee Democrat* (September 7, 1975).
      Review of CRI SD342. Remarks that the best of the pieces is the *Duo for
      Viola and Piano* and describes it as being "in the form of a contrasting,
      sometimes antagonist dialogue."

59   "New Works." *Music Journal* (May 1965).
      Review of the world premiere of *Concert Overture*. Described as "an effective piece of non-programmatic, absolute music, modern in style, but not unduly dissonant."

60   "New York." *Classical* (January 1991).
      Brief report of the significance of Bazelon's hobby of spending Saturdays at the racetrack to the genesis of two of his compositions, *Churchill Downs Concerto* and the recently premiered *Sunday Silence*. Includes the same comment as 92. Includes a photograph of Bazelon and his wife at Churchill Downs.

61   "North/South Consonance." *The New York Times* (September 11, 1989).
      Announcement of a concert featuring a work by Irwin Bazelon.

62   "Obituary Index." *Notes* (June 1996).
      An entry, in a list of obituaries, noting the death of Bazelon, giving the date of death, the age of the composer and the city in which he died.

63   "Opus Music Reviews." *Opus* (June 1987).
      Review by A.K. of CRI SD532 which includes *Imprints* and *Five Pieces for Piano*. Describes the composer as tempering "his drive toward angularity with an impulse toward the colorfully lyrical." *Imprints* is described as making "full use of the piano's compass, dynamic range, and timbral resources, including forays into the instrument's innards, which, sparing at first, increase as the work progresses, and enhance rather than detract from the music's sense of inexorable development." The *Five Pieces* are described as "brief attractive works" with "masterfully transparent counterpoint."

64   "Percussive Music." *The New York Herald Tribune* (March 18, 1950).
      Review by T.M.S. of the world premiere of *Sonata No. 2 for Piano*. Notes the occasional "bright spots of decorated counterpoint" but criticises the work for stylistic inconsistency, jumping too frequently from "romantic to fiercely dissonant to bombastic".

65   "Premieres." *Music Educators Journal* (March 1976).
      Gives brief details, in a list of premieres, about the world premiere of *A Quiet Piece ... for a Violent Time*.

66   "Premieres." *Music Educators Journal* (September 1977).
      Gives brief details, in a list of premieres, about the world premiere of *Concatenations*.

67   "Premieres." *Music Educators Journal* (February 1980).
      Gives brief details, in a list of premieres, about the world premiere of *De-
      Tonations for Brass Quintet and Orchestra*.

68   "Premieres." *Music Journal* (April 1964).
      Gives brief details of the world premieres of the *Duo for Viola and Piano*
      and the *Brass Quintet*.

69   "Premieres." *Music Journal* (June 1966).
      Gives brief details of the world premiere of *Excursion for Orchestra*.

70   "Premieres." *Music Journal* (December 1975).
      Item about the world premiere of *A Quiet Piece ... for a Violent Time*.
      Includes brief details about other works by Bazelon describing both his
      freelance activities and his symphonic output.

71   "Premieres." *Symphony News* (December 1975).
      Gives details, in a list of premieres, of the world premiere of *A Quiet
      Piece ... for a Violent Time*.

72   "Present-day Music Given at Columbia." *The New York Times* (April 2,
      1951).
      Review by C.H. of the world premiere of *Five Pieces for Piano*. Assesses
      it as the best work by Bazelon so far but criticises its forward momentum
      in terms of its rhythmic impulse and its contrapuntal style.

73   "Program to Feature Premiere." *Greenfield (Mass.) Recorder* (August 1,
      1973).
      Article anticipating the world premiere of *Duo for Viola and Piano* in the
      Mohawk Trail Concerts. Includes some biographical material with
      references to the NBC-TV news theme, to his interest in horse racing and
      the racetrack where, in a microcosm of all aspects of life, "hope, anxiety,
      success, joy, failure, anticipation are capsulized in a two-minute ride," to
      his studying composition with Hindemith and Milhaud and, erroneously,
      to his "early career as a professional baseball player." Includes a
      photograph.

74   "A Quiet Piece ... for a Violent Time." *High Fidelity / Musical America*
      (March 1976).
      Notes the world premiere of *A Quiet Piece ... for a Violent Time*.

75   "Rebecca LaBrecque." *Musical America* (July 1979).
      Review of the world premiere of *Imprints . . . on Ivory and Strings*.
      Described as "a kaleidoscope of evocative passages and special effects

that never seemed gimmicky." Also includes favourable comments on Rebecca LaBrecque's technique and understanding of contemporary music.

76   "Record Review." *Consumer Reports* (January 1973).
Review of CRI SD287. Describes *Symphony No. 5* as "intense and passionate, containing elements of atonal technique blended with ... a 'synthetic' jazz spirit. The first movement is brooding and introspective, the second and third movements have characteristics of dance, and the final movement is a stern and ultimately serene section that grows out of the third movement. This symphony is a tough and sometimes disturbing one, and it reveals Bazelon as a composer with much to say about our present condition."

77   "Review Section." *London College of Music Magazine* (1985).
Review of *Suite for Marimba* published by Novello. Described as "musically intriguing" and "challenging" with a "quirky originality" that is "unmistakably American."

78   "Ruth Strassman in First Recital." *The New York Times* (October 17, 1950).
Review by R.P. of the debut recital of Ruth Strassman which included four pieces from *Piano Suite for Young People*. Briefly discusses the witty character of the pieces and the effectiveness with which they achieved their objective.

79   "Ruth Strassman." *Musical Leader* (October 16, 1950).
Review by R.E. of the debut recital of Ruth Strassman which included four pieces from *Piano Suite for Young People*. Described as "well made" and "subtly suggestive of their titles."

80   "Season Premieres, 1984-1985." *Symphony Magazine* (October / November 1984).
Gives details, in a list of premieres, of the world premiere of *Symphony Concertante*. Includes the names of the soloists.

81   "Solomon, ISO To Record Bazelon Work." *The Indianapolis Star* (November 25, 1971).
Announcement of the recording of *Symphony No. 5* by the Indianapolis Symphony Orchestra and *Churchill Downs* for release by Composers Recording Inc. with the help of the Ford Foundation, Boosey and Hawkes and private sources. *Churchill Downs* is described by Bazelon as "a wild, rhythmic, jazzy score that will make a good contrast" with "my more lyrical Symphony."

82   "Sound Dreams." *The Providence Journal Bulletin* (March 5, 1985).
        Review of a performance of *Sound Dreams*. Notes that "an ominous roll
        of the side drum introduced Bazelon's *Sound Dreams*. This echo of a
        march to the scaffold, in combination with lyric snatches and a variety of
        other fragmented elements ... served to emphasize the piece's
        apparitional title, occasionally with some wit."

83   "Steppin' Out." *ASCAP in Action* (Fall 1984).
        Details of the world premiere of *Quintessentials*.

84   "Steppin' Out." *ASCAP in Action* (Fall 1985).
        Details of the world premiere of *Symphony Concertante*.

85   "Stravinsky Two Nights." *Indianapolis News* (December 1, 1971).
        News item anticipating a performance of *Symphony No. 5*.

86   "Three Premieres at One Concert." *The New York Herald Tribune*
        (March 22, 1965).
        Review by W.L. of the world premiere of *Concert Overture*. Described
        as "inventive in its development" and "robust and bright in sound."

87   "Your Words Alone Are a Symphony." *The Courier-Journal* (May 23,
        1966).
        Brief news item noting Bazelon's presence in Louisville to oversee the
        recording of his *Short Symphony* by the Louisville Orchestra at the time
        of the 92nd Kentucky Derby. Overwhelmed by the experience of seeing
        his first Derby, Bazelon announced his intention of composing a
        Churchill Downs Concerto. Includes some detailed information on how
        much and on what horse Bazelon bet on the 92nd Kentucky Derby.

88   "Visiting." *The Seattle Times* (February 20, 1966).
        News item anticipating the world premiere of *Dramatic Movement for
        Orchestra*. Includes brief details of social events preceding the concert.
        Includes a photograph.

89   Adler, Renata. "Not Better Than Even, But Better." *The New York Times*
        (June 23, 1968).
        Review of the television documentary *Survival 1967*. Comments
        adversely on all aspects of the programme apart from the music of Irwin
        Bazelon.

90   Allenby, David. "William Moersch." *Musical Opinion* (June 1987).
        Review of the debut London recital of William Moersch which included
        a performance of *Suite for Marimba*. Comments favourably upon the

work's "spiky angularity" and on the "punchy rhythmic writing of the third movement."

91   Anderson, E. Ruth. "Irwin Bazelon." *Contemporary American Composers, A Biographical Dictionary,* GK Hall Co., Boston, Massachusetts (1976).
Dictionary entry on Bazelon. Gives information on date and place of birth, education (studying composition with Milhaud and Bloch) and awards. Bazelon is described as a full-time composer who also teaches "a course on music for films at the School of Visual Arts" in New York. Includes a selected list of works with details of first performances from 1947 to 1971. It includes an unknown *String Quartet with amplified contrabass* dated 1967 which may have become the later IB83 *For Tuba ... with strings attached* (1982).

92   Anderson, Susan Heller. "A Horse of a Different Tonal Color." *The New York Times* (September 26, 1990).
Brief news item anticipating the world premiere of *Sunday Silence.* Includes comments by the composer on the relationship of the piece to the racehorse after which the work was named. Bazelon draws a distinction between a piece that is evocative rather than descriptive. The way the horse runs is compared to his music in terms of rhythmic energy. Includes references to Bazelon's passion for horse racing and that an earlier composition, *Churchill Downs,* is named after the Kentucky race track.

93   Atkinson, Brooks. "Idolators of New York Raise Cain." *The New York Times* (November 23, 1962).
Column with an unusual juxtaposition of comments by Bazelon, anticipating the first performance of his *Short Symphony, Testimonial to a Big City,* and by Prof. J. Mitchell Morse of Pennsylvania State University suggesting, as part of his interpretation of the mythology of the Old Testament, that the first city was founded by Cain. Although the author devotes more space to his biblical theme, he does record Bazelon as saying that "because I deal in the world of sound, I find the city not a human wilderness, but an exciting human jungle: a jungle belching forth a cascade of brassy discords, rebellious mutterings and cross rhythms...." Bazelon also states that "without the city and its magnetic vitality, I would not have found my "own sounds" and developed my personal style of composition." Also notes that winnings at the Aqueduct enabled him to record the *Concert Ballet,* using members of the New York Philharmonic, which helped him obtain a performance of *Testimonial to a Big City.*

94   Barela, Margeret Mary. "Premiere of Bazelon piece." *The Berkshire Eagle* (April 30, 1985).
Review of the world premiere of *Symphony Concertante*. Compares the work with Bartok's *The Miraculous Mandarin* noting differences between the approach of the two composers to continuity. Comments on the scoring, the use of instruments and the melodic and rhythmic content. Discusses the origins of the musical inspiration in Bazelon's experience of city life and its effect on musical tension. Also comments on the soloist's performance.

95   Barela, Margaret Mary. "World premiere in Williamstown of 'old' symphony by Irwin Bazelon." *The Berkshire Eagle* (April 25, 1985).
Article about the forthcoming world premiere of *Symphony Concertante* by the Berkshire Symphony Orchestra. The conductor Julius Heygi is praised by Bazelon for his support of American contemporary music. There are comments on the unorthodox scoring of the work and its rhythmic difficulties. Also includes an account of Bazelon's deafness (its childhood origin in scarlet fever and its eventual cure by an operation in his 30s) and its significance for the composer suggesting that, "by listening to, and then giving voice to, the violence and aggressive feelings that emerged in the silence of his affliction, he has come to terms with them. Consequently, he has given to his audience a reflection of the tense and restless city life he sees in this age." Quotes some typical Bazelon comments on the relationship between his music and American city life: "My roots are in the city. My music exhibits an enormous rhythmic propulsion. It's not at all minimalistic, not meant to hypnotize. My music is me. You may not like it, but you won't be bored by it." Includes an account of Bazelon's compositional career, studying music at DePaul University, then composition with Hindemith and Milhaud and the composer's strong "inner drive for self-expression." Describes the turning point in his career, a review of his *Short Symphony* by Paul Hume in the Washington Post (164) that led to the publication of his music by Boosey and Hawkes. Also describes the award of the Serge Koussevitzky prize in 1982 and the commission of *Fusions*. Notes the preponderance of works for brass and percussion, a sound that Bazelon views as "the 20th-century equivalent of the 19th-century string quartet." Discusses the relationship between the composer of film music and the serious composer quoting Bazelon as saying, "I chose carefully so that the ideas I tried out could be carried over to my concert works. There was no translation necessary, so there was no need for compromise. I've had the opportunity to hear my sounds, to find out what works and what doesn't." Other subjects discussed include the wordplay often found in the titles of Bazelon's pieces, with references to *Re-Percussions, De-Tonations, For Tuba with Strings Attached, Triple Play, Tides,* and

Fourscore, and the composer's activities as a lecturer, although the article begins with Bazelon describing himself as an anomaly, "one of the few composers who does not teach in a college or university setting." The article ends with the hope that the forthcoming performance will be "yet another step towards breaking the "violent silence," towards being heard, accepted and eventually acknowledged for giving voice to the spirit of this age." Includes a photograph.

96   Bell, Richard. "Empire Brass aims to please." *The Boston Globe* (January 20, 1981).
      Review of the world premiere of *Cross-Currents*. Notes that the work "endeavoured to take the pulse of the big city" and was full of "discontinuities, nasty loud surprises, hubbub and unusual uses of the instrument."

97   Belt, Byron. "A Racy Concerto." *Long Island Press* (May 7, 1972).
      Review of a recording of *Churchill Downs Concerto* and *Symphony No. 5,* launched by Composers Recordings on the same day as the Kentucky Derby. Using a racing analogy the reviewer states that "Bazelon's current entry in the recordings sweepstakes is a sure winner." Despite the composer's own comments in the sleeve notes on the "restless surge of supercharged city life," the reviewer finds that "the basic atmosphere of the symphony is one of mystery and a profound melancholy." Also includes some biographical material and a description of Bazelon's activities as a professional composer. Bazelon is described as "a composer with a tremendous respect for the craft of his trade" and quoted as saying "I apply the same techniques, the same fire and integrity to the slightest toothpaste commercial as to my most complex symphonic movement." Of his music Bazelon says "I like fast over slow, high over low, loudness to softness - I'm a dramatic composer. My music snarls rather than caresses, but I'm not afraid to write a melody." Bazelon is also quoted as saying "I was seduced by the sound of the Chicago Symphony under Frederick Stock when I was just 10, and I've been the happy victim of that seduction ever since" giving a remarkably early date of 1934 for this event, which is not confirmed in other sources by his comments, where it is usually described as occurring after Bazelon began a career as jazz pianist in a dance band. Includes a reproduction of the woodcut from the record cover, a portrait of the composer by his artist-wife.

98   Belt, Byron. "Churchill Downs is a winner." *Courier-Journal and Times* (May 7, 1972).
      Review of a recording of *Churchill Downs Concerto* and *Symphony No. 5* launched by Composers Recordings on the same day as the Kentucky

Derby. (There are differences between this review and 97). *Churchill Downs* is described as "entertaining" and *Symphony No. 5* as "brooding and darkly beautiful." Also refers to *Short Symphony No. 2*. Includes a description of Bazelon's professional activities as a composer.

99   Bennett, Richard Rodney. "Irwin Bazelon." *Contemporary Composers,* ed. Brian Morton and Pamela Collins, St James Press, Chicago (1992).
Extensive dictionary entry on Bazelon. It remarks upon his "remarkable individuality" and his "isolation from the musical establishment." Discusses his composition studies with Hindemith, who Bazelon found "lacking in warmth and understanding," and with Milhaud, who was "much more stimulating and sympathetic," notes some of the early influences upon his compositional style and describes his early works as "competent and disciplined" but lacking a "truly personal voice." Describes his early years living in the stimulating, vibrant atmosphere of New York where he worked for seven years as a railroad reservations clerk. Explains the nature of an inner-ear affliction causing partial deafness which, when eventually successfully treated by an ear surgeon, had a dramatic effect upon the composer as "the violent silent world inside" him suddenly "erupted" as he "came out of" his "shell." Discusses the nature of the music written for television commercials, documentary films and plays, noting Bazelon's commitment to a contemporary musical language in these short fragments of music. Describes the evolution of a highly personal style in Bazelon's concert works through a combination of atonal melodic and harmonic elements of a quasi-serial origin, a stylised use of jazz idioms without a rhythm section and an "extraordinary rhythmic energy" typically creating either a fast movement characterised by "violent dislocations and cross rhythms" that suggests a "piece of atonal modern jazz" or slower music that tends to be of a "brooding, unlyrical" nature. References to specific works include his symphonic output, his writing for unconventional chamber combinations and his more recent writing for the voice and the new and "typically unpredictable element of lyricism" it has introduced into his music. Ends by emphasising Bazelon's uniquely personal voice and its origin in "his own nervous, sometimes violent interior world." Includes a list of works up to 1986.

100   Berger, Arthur. "League of Composers." *The New York Herald Tribune* (April 7, 1954).
Review of a concert that included movements from *Piano Suite for Young People.* The *Cowboy Tune* is described as standing out "for a charm and grace in its two-part writing."

101   Berliner, Milton. "Ricci Makes Dazzling Display of Paganini." *The Washington Daily News* (December 5, 1962).
Review of the world premiere of *Short Symphony No. 2, Testimonial to a Big City*. Describes the work as concise and terse. Discusses the "clever use of instruments" to conjure up "a vision of the city" from the "quiet early hours of the morning" to "a sort of Slaughter-on-Tenth-Avenue finale, replete with staccato drums" representing "the violence of the city." Also comments on Bazelon's conducting.

102   Biancolli, Louis. "Americas Have Their Day in Two Carnegie Concerts." *The World-Telegram* (March 22, 1965).
Review of the world premiere of the *Concert Overture* by the Orchestra of America. Described as "loud and strenuous," and noting that "Bazelon has much to say," the reviewer asked to "hear something else of his, something built around a solid idea with places of its own to go."

103   Bignell, Rob. "Commissioned composer in residence on campus." *The Student Voice* (May 2, 1985).
Article anticipating Bazelon being composer-in-residence at the University of Wisconsin, River Falls in May 1985. Includes comments on the inspiration of the city, on Bazelon's writing for percussion, anticipating the world premiere of *Fourscore* (with references to *Propulsions, Double Crossings, Triple Play* and *Cross-Currents*), and on his writing for brass and wind, anticipating a performance of the *Woodwind Quintet*. Includes brief biographical details.

104   Bohm, Jerome. "Pianist in Debut." *The New York Herald Tribune* (October 17, 1950).
Review of the debut recital by Ruth Strassman that included four pieces from the *Piano Suite for Young People*. Described as "unpretentious and entertaining."

105   Brown, Royal. "Film Musings." *Fanfare* (November / December 1995).
Obituary. Comments concentrate on Bazelon's book *Knowing the Score: Notes on Film Music* which is described as "one of the best works" on film music containing "probing and sometimes scathing analyses."

106   Buchwald, Art. "Cultural Collateral." *The Washington Post* (December 10, 1962).
Article about Bazelon and the world premiere of his *Short Symphony, Testimonial to a Big City* in Washington. It is an extended and witty account of the confusion an American composer caused in a New York bank by asking for a personal loan and offering three of his symphonies as collateral. It ends by remarking that "American composers may be

poor, but that doesn't mean they can't have a little fun." Its humour makes it one of the most powerful statements of a frequently recurring comment by Bazelon, the need for society to make adequate financial provision for its creative artists. It is also a metaphorical discussion of the position of the artist in society and the problems of evaluating art in terms defined by a society dominated by commercial concerns.

107   Buchwald, Art. "When the chips are down, composer can't bank on getting a loan." American Composers Alliance Bulletin (1963 no. 1).
        As 106. Reprinted from the New York Herald Tribune.

108   Burke, Richard. *Fanfare* (September/October 1994).
        Review of Albany Troy 101. Describes the overall effect of the music as "powerful" and "very direct." Notes that the serial and jazz elements in the works "are part of an urban landscape that his work reflects." Also includes brief specific comments on *Memories of a Winter Childhood, Symphony No. 8½, Prelude to Hart Crane's The Bridge, Alliances* and *Four ... Parts of a World.*

109   Butler, Henry. "Symphony No. 5." *Indianapolis Symphony Orchestra Program Notes* (May 8, 1969).
        Programme note for the world premiere of *Symphony No. 5.* Includes biographical details on how the composer supports himself by playing the horses, receiving foundation grants and composing music for industrial documentaries. Gives brief details of Bazelon's artistic career, composition teachers and important orchestral performances. Quotes a detailed description of each movement supplied by the composer as well as more general observations on style including the free use of 12-tone techniques and a "synthetic" jazz spirit "characterised more by rhythmic vitality than formalised jazz techniques." Ends with a description of the compositional force of the music being a response to the composer's experience of city life but also states that the symphony has no "programmatic intent."

110   Butler, Henry. "Symphony No. 5." *Indianapolis Symphony Orchestra Program Notes* (December 2, 1971).
        Programme note for a performance of *Symphony No. 5.* Largely the same as the one used for the world premiere (109) omitting the detailed description of the content of individual movements. The biographical material has been re-arranged to include comments by the composer taken from Newsweek (6).

111   Butterworth, Neil. "Irwin Bazelon." *A Dictionary of American Composers*, Garland, New York (1984).

Dictionary entry on Bazelon. Includes information on his education and his studying composition with Milhaud and advanced analysis with Ernest Bloch. An extensive list of orchestral and chamber works from 1950 to 1982 includes an unknown *Sound Play for six players* (1982) which might have been an earlier version of IB84 *Fusions* (1983) and a projected *Jubilee Overture* which may have formed the basis of IB89 *Symphony No. 8 for Strings* (1986). Also includes references to Bazelon's music for theatre and television and to his book *Knowing the Score: Notes on Film Music.*

112   Cariaga, Daniel. "Newman Group in Concert." *Los Angeles Times* (November 19, 1973).
Review of a production by the Gloria Newman Dance Theater Company that included a piece called *Orbits.* The choreography is described as matching "Irwin Bazelon's terse musical line point for point."

113   Church, Francis. *The Courier-Journal* (April 30, 1972).
Review of record release of *Churchill Downs* and *Symphony No. 5* on CRI SD287. *Churchill Downs* is described as "one of the most successful mergers of rock-jazz-classical music" known to the reviewer whereas *Symphony No. 5* is criticised for being preoccupied "with technique at the expense of ideas." Also includes some information on the composer's success in winning money at the Kentucky Derby.

114   Cohen, Barry. "A Memorial Concert to Irwin Bazelon." *The Music Connoisseur* (1995, vol. 3, no. 4).
Review of the Bazelon Memorial Concert in New York in 1995. Describes the composer as having plenty of "spirit" and that the pieces performed in the concert were "uncompromising." Describes Bazelon's musical personality as "individualistic" noting flashes "of wit" and "of real beauty," the work of a man "with a tough exterior and an inner sensitivity." Discusses the eloquence of *Alliances* noting that its "long, often fading cello lines are punctuated meaningfully by the piano." Comments more briefly on *Re-Percussions, Triple Play* and the *Woodwind Quintet.* Includes a brief account of Bazelon's output, referring to his symphonic composition and to his authorship of *Knowing the Score: Notes on Film Music.* Includes a photograph.

115   Cohn, Arthur. "In excellent health - the Louisville Project." *American Record Guide* (February 1968).
Review of the LP issue of *Symphony No. 2, Testament to a Big City* as part of a survey of a number of recordings. Comments favourably upon the "compact drama that pervades the slow movement" but criticises the faster outer sections as "lacking in the necessary balance of tension and

resolution." Also discusses the absence of any substantiation of the promised "programmatic pictorialism" of the subtitle while suggesting that the music would be suitable for "a film score but lacks the necessary substances for a symphony."

116   Cook, David. "Bazelon Works Are Listenable." *Tallahassee Democrat* (May 14, 1972).
Review of CRI SD287 which includes *Symphony No. 5* and *Churchill Downs*. Describes *Symphony No. 5* as "a rather mysterious work" with sounds giving "a feeling of the city" and *Churchill Downs* as an "exhilarating experience."

117   Cook, David. "Composers Recording Inc." *Tallahassee Democrat* (February 2, 1975).
Review of CRI SD327. Suggests that *Propulsions* would be more entertaining to watch than to hear due to its large army of instruments. Describes the *Brass Quintet* as "a substantial piece of music leaving a strong impression."

118   Cox, David Harold. "Irwin Bazelon." *The New Grove Dictionary of American Music* edited by H. Wiley Hitchcock and Stanley Sadie (1986).
Dictionary entry on Bazelon. Includes information on his education, composition studies with Milhaud, fellowships at the MacDowell Colony and other awards. Includes references to *Propulsions, Brass Quintet, Cross-Currents, De-Tonations, Churchill Downs* and *A Quiet Piece for a Violent Time*. Describes the power of Bazelon's music as arising from "his energetic personality and his experience of city life" and the way in which the rhythmic, melodic and harmonic elements of his musical language convey "the nervous tension and energy of the city." Discusses Bazelon's "extensive and complex treatment" of thematic material in which a "process of continual variation and transformation" is created by various methods including "patterns of pitch relationships and loosely applied serial procedures." Includes a comprehensive list of works to 1983.

119   Cox, David Harold. "The Music of Bazelon." *Percussive Notes* (August 1990).
Article on Bazelon's music for percussion. Includes brief biographical details and an account of how the composer's experience of city life led to the development of a powerful and original rhythmic language. Discusses the Concerto for Percussion, *Propulsions,* describing it as "challenging, uncompromising and original" and commenting on its instrumentation and on its use of "sonority to create energy and drive" with a technique, perhaps "influenced by Varèse," in which sound is

"shaped by its volume and timbre and thrust forward in a series of jagged attacks by its rhythm." Notes the tension between "silence and the forces opposing it" and its possible reflection of "an Ivesian duality between the inner and outer worlds of man" as is perhaps implicit in the title *A Quiet Piece ... for a Violent Time.* Comments on a number of works that combine the sounds of brass and percussion including *Double Crossings, Triple Play* and *Cross-Currents,* discussing the musical content of the latter work in some detail. The combination and eventual synthesis of unequal opposing forces is explored further in a discussion of the musical content and the formal structure of *Partnership for Timpani and Marimba.* Bazelon's use of formal structures involving a sequence of pitch-centres is demonstrated by reference to the *Suite for Marimba.* A musical example from the work illustrates the "kind of melodic apotheosis" which Bazelon often used as the "ultimate objective of the musical design." Also discusses Bazelon's writing for percussion quartet, describing the formal structure of *Concatenations* and the relationship between the writing for solo viola and percussion and the structure of *Fourscore +2* illustrating with musical examples the underlying motivic organisation of the work and providing a tabular analysis of the third movement in order to establish Bazelon's "firm grasp of the architectonic principles of music." Includes a list of works for percussion written between 1974 and 1987. Includes a photograph.

120   Cox, David Harold. "A World of Violent Silence." *The Musical Times* (October 1982).
Article reviewing the achievement of the composer in his sixtieth year and anticipating performances of *Propulsions* and *Churchill Downs* at the Royal Northern College of Music, Manchester, England. Describes the artistic inspiration Bazelon finds in city life, found in microcosm at the racetrack, quoting the composer's comment that "the alternations of mood, colour and dramatic flair are a direct expression of the constant changes of pace, the rhythmic beat of life in the big metropolis." Also notes that the power of the music is derived from the underlying tensions of a temperament that lives in "a world of violent silence" and the origins of this experience in a medical condition which had given rise to hearing difficulties during the composer's youth. Gives brief biographical details of Bazelon's early life and musical training. Includes detailed discussion of Bazelon's musical idiom and of the driving force of rhythm in Bazelon's musical language. Suggests that "the nervous energy imbuing his music is produced by a rhythmic language of a breadth and sophistication that calls to mind great masters of rhythmic freedom in the 20th century such as Bartók and Varèse. The stylistic character of *Propulsions* and *Churchill Downs* is discussed in some depth. Examines the composer's use of serial procedures, the wide-ranging character of

his thematic material, his preference for the sounds of wind, brass and percussion and the construction of formal shapes determined by the succession of textural patterns and tempo sequences. Also notes that "patterns of pitch relationships and loosely applied serial procedures are found in the earlier works" illustrated with reference to the *Brass Quintet* which opposes two groups of three pitches (C, D flat and F to A, B flat and D) and *Symphony No. 5* which, as well as using 12-note techniques, although not in a strict way, also employs a concept of "negative tonality" in that "each of the four movements strives to reach the pitch-centre C established at the beginning of the work, but each time it is rejected." Refers to a number of other Bazelon works including the second and sixth symphonies, *Double Crossings, Triple Play, Cross-Currents, De-Tonations* and *A Quiet Piece for a Violent Time.* Ends with brief references to parallels with the significance of the city in other arts. Includes a photograph.

121   Crist, Judith. "'Merry Wives of Windsor' Staged at Stratford, Conn." *The New York Herald Tribune* (July 9, 1959).
Review of the American Shakespeare Festival's production of *The Merry Wives of Windsor* staged by John Houseman and Jack Landau with music by Bazelon. Describes the music as a "pleasing prelude and unobtrusive occasional accompaniment."

122   Croan, Robert. "Ensemble Opening." *Pittsburgh Post-Gazette* (October 23, 1984).
Review of the world premiere of *Fusions.* Notes that the work "exploits color and dynamic materials with conventional means that lead to original, not-always-conventional results."

123   Cullen, Sandy. "Symphony, Soloists Triumph." *The Patriot News* (December 6, 1989).
Review of the world premiere of *Memories of a Winter Childhood.* Notes that the work is an elegy to the composer's mother who died in 1980. Described as creating "a mood of anxiousness in which fleeting fragments of emotions spanning a lifetime seem to hang in suspension, as in a time of grief when a person who has suffered a loss feels mostly numbness. There are indications of angry frustration which give way to an emotionally-charged ending. The concluding musical collage combines a 1940s boogie-woogie piano solo with an array of percussion and a lullaby performed by the strings while a solo trumpet plays 'Ramona,' his mother's favourite song from the 1920s."

124   Davis, Peter. "Two Composers Lead Their Own Works." *The New York Times* (December 7, 1976).

Review of a concert in Carnegie Recital Hall that included the *Brass Quintet, Duo for Viola and Piano* and the world premiere of *Double Crossings*. Discusses the distinctive and aggressive style of Bazelon's music, assessing in particular the impact of its rhythmic energy. The other composer whose music featured in the concert was Claire Polin.

125   Delacoma, Wynne. "Classical: Ensemble Spotlights Double Bass." *The Chicago Sun-Times* (November 9, 1992).
Review of the world premiere of *Prelude to Hart Crane's The Bridge*. Notes that the composer was from Chicago and was now based in New York. Describes a "sense of hushed expectation created by individual, long-sustained melodic fragments" which sounded like an appropriate introduction to the longer work planned by the composer.

126   Delacoma, Wynne. "Irwin Bazelon, 73; Composer Wrote Music for Orchestras, Film, TV." *The Chicago Sun-Times* (August 5, 1995).
Obituary. Notes that the composer was born in Evanston, was a graduate of Senn High School, and earned Bachelor's and Master's degrees from DePaul University before studying composition with Hindemith and Milhaud. It includes brief information on his work as a professional composer of music for films and TV documentaries and that he was the author of a book on film music, *Knowing the Score: Notes on Film Music*. Notes that Bazelon had been working on his tenth symphony, a large-scale piece for orchestra and chorus based on the writings of Hart Crane and that two years previously the Chicago String Ensemble had given the world premiere of his *Prelude to Hart Crane's The Bridge*. His musical style is described as "eclectic."

127   Ditsky, John. *Fanfare* (March/April 1987).
Review of CRI SD532 which included the *Five Pieces for Piano* and *Imprints*. Described as being "thorny explorations of the instrument's possibilities" but "worth the determined listening the music demands."

128   Donnelly, Tom. "That's What Horse Races Make." *The Washington Daily News* (December 3, 1962).
Article anticipating the world premiere of the *Short Symphony, Testimonial to a Big City*. It includes comments by Bazelon on the difficulty of persuading conductors to perform new music and on the lack of financial support for serious composers. Bazelon describes how he supports himself by writing music for TV commercials, industrial films, opening music for the Armstrong Circle Theater and the NBC news theme. He remarks that "in a few advertising agencies there are a handful of men with taste" who "commission original music" and "don't try to tell me how to write it." Noting that "Madison Avenue and the heads of

some of those giant corporations are indirectly subsidizing serious composers," he remarks that "I don't suppose it ever occurs to the chairman of the board of the Peerless Pickle Company that he's helping some man he never heard of to eat while writing a string quartet." Bazelon also describes how he used his racetrack winnings to produce a tape recording of his *Concert Ballet* in order to introduce his music to the conductor of the National Symphony Orchestra, Howard Mitchell. The article concludes with Bazelon's assessment of the cost to him, about seven hundred dollars, of having his symphony performed, remarking that "even if nobody likes my symphony, it'll be worth it."

129   Drone, J. "American composer update." *Pan Pipes of Sigma Alpha* (1983 no. 2).
       Review of the 1982 premieres, performances, publications and recordings of Irwin Bazelon.

130   Dufour, Charles. "Women artists well received." *New Orleans States-Item* (October 29, 1975).
       Review of the world premiere of *A Quiet Piece ... for a Violent Time.* Discusses a concentration on orchestral colour rather than melodic line. Remarks that "it was not without interest."

131   Dyer, Richard. "Disturbing pieces dominate program." *The Boston Globe* (November 9, 1988).
       Review of a performance of *Legends and Love Letters.* Notes "an attractive streak of nostalgia" and a "vividly immediate response to the poet's response to nature." Includes comments on the singing of Joan Heller.

132   Ellis, Stephen. "The Want List." *Fanfare* (November/December 1991).
       Brief review of LE331 which includes *Symphony No. 8.* Described as a major score.

133   Ewen, David. "Irwin Bazelon." *American Composers, A Biographical Dictionary,* Hale, London (1983).
       Extensive dictionary entry on Bazelon. Describes Bazelon as both a "functional" composer writing music for television and films and a "serious" composer whose concert works are highly esteemed. Notes the cross-fertilisation between the two aspects of his creativity revealed by his "sensitive ear for unusual instrumental colorations" and by the way popular elements "sometimes intrude into his serious writing." Describes the young Bazelon as "shy and introspective" due to a semideaf left ear caused by scarlet fever. Notes his sporting prowess and the comparatively late dawning of a "musical consciousness" after hearing a

concert by the Chicago Symphony Orchestra. Describes his early musical studies on the piano with Irving Harris and Magdalen Massmann and composition at DePaul University with Leon Stein acknowledging his "powerful influence in awakening Bazelon's ambition to become a composer," and then the varying significance of his further studies with Hindemith, Milhaud and Ernest Bloch. Also describes Bazelon settling in New York from 1948, working as a railroad reservations clerk for seven years while he attempted to get himself established as a composer, and the importance of a successful operation by an ear surgeon to cure his inner-ear affliction and its impact upon the composer's personality as the "violent, silent world inside" him then "erupted." Gives details of Bazelon's work as a professional composer writing music for commercials, naming the first three, Ipana, Buitoni and Noxzema, the incidental music for two productions by the American Shakepeare Theater, and his music for television and films including *Survival 1967, Wilma, What Makes Sammy Run?* and the NBC-TV news theme. A detailed description of Bazelon's serious compositions includes references to early performances of *String Quartet No. 2, Piano Sonatas Nos. 1 and 2, Suite for Clarinet, Cello and Piano, Five Pieces for Piano, Ballet Suite, Movimento da Camera* and the *Chamber Symphony for Seven Instruments.* The events leading up to the first performance of the *Short Symphony, Testimony to a Big City* are recounted introducing both Bazelon's fascination for the racetrack and the inspirational force of the city and its influence upon the style of Bazelon's music in a description which emphasises its freedom of expression and its "muscular strength." References to further performances of works in the 1960s include *Symphonies Nos. 1, 5* and *6, Dramatic Movement, Excursions, Symphony Concertante* and *Dramatic Fanfare.* Also notes the major works since 1970 and their first performances including *Churchill Downs, Woodwind Quintet, A Quiet Piece ... for a Violent Time, Double Crossings, Sound Dreams* and *De-Tonations.* Includes details of Bazelon's marriage to Cecile Gray Bazelon, various awards received by the composer, and his book on film music, *Knowing the Score: Notes on Film Music.* Ends by quoting the composer's own comments on his music. Includes a list of main works from 1947 to 1978.

134   Fain, Kenneth. "Meet the Composer." *The Cultural Post* (National Endowment for the Arts) (September/October 1977).
Article about the American Music Center's program "Meet the Composer." Includes comments by Bazelon on the objectives of the program. Also describes how a "Meet the Composer" grant enabled the Boehm Woodwind Quintette to learn, perform and subsequently record the *Woodwind Quintet.*

135   Finn, Robert. "World premiere highlights concert." *Cleveland Plain Dealer* (February 11, 1983).
       Review of the world premiere of *Re-Percussions*. Comments on the dense textures, dissonant idiom and "sonorous commanding gestures" creating "attractive and virtuosic music."

136   Fisher, George.   *Notes: Quarterly Journal of the Music Library Association* (December 1996).
       Review of the publication of *Four ... Parts of a World* by Theodore Presser in 1994. Compares the work with a song-cycle by Allen Shearer which also sets the poetry of Wallace Stevens. Refers to a number of other works that are settings of texts by the poet. Notes that both Bazelon and Shearer "adopt a conservative approach" to the setting of the text "favoring a syllabic setting" that "respects the natural accentuation of the words." Discusses other similarities between the works including the manipulation of a chromatic language and the technical difficulty of the vocal part. The fact that both cycles end with a setting of *The Candle a Saint* enables the reviewer to compare the approach of the two composers directly, noting especially the radically different tempi chosen for the start of the song (Bazelon's is fast whereas Shearer's is slow) and the character of the opening vocal phrase (Bazelon's is angular whilst Shearer's is smooth).

137   Ford, Elizabeth.   "After Concerts Are Over, 'Testimonial' Melodies Linger On." *The Washington Post* (December 6, 1962).
       Report on the party given after the world premiere of *Short Symphony, Testimonial to a Big City* hosted by Judge and Mrs David Lionel Bazelon at their Washington home. Guests included James Jones (author of *From Here to Eternity)* and his wife, life-long friends of the Bazelons, and the composer's parents and brother and sister-in-law.

138   Gagnard, Frank. "Dome to Rock Again." *New Orleans Times* (October 25, 1975).
       Brief news report anticipating the world premiere of *A Quiet Piece ... for a Violent Time.*

139   Gagnard, Frank.   "He Wrote the Music For TV Newscasts." *New Orleans Times* (October 22, 1975).
       Article anticipating the world premiere of *A Quiet Piece ... for a Violent Time* by the New Orleans Symphony. Describes the clear intentions of the "no-nonsense" titles of a number of other works: *Short Symphony, Dramatic Movement for Orchestra, Excursion for Orchestra, Concert Overture* and *Churchill Downs*. The latter work is used to introduce Bazelon's love of horse racing and the finale of *Dramatic Movement for*

Orchestra is described as an attempt "to evoke horses pounding down the stretch at Aqueduct." [The origin of this comment is probably 7 but it is contradicted by many of the composer's other statements about his music not being programmatic in intent]. Notes Bazelon's various professional activities, the composer of the NBC-TV news theme, of incidental music for the American Shakespeare Festival Theater, and of the film score for Jules Dassin's documentary about the Six-Day War, *Survival 1967*.

140   Gagnard, Frank. "Symphony Concert Has Much Going On." *The Times-Picayune* (October 30, 1975).
Review of the world premiere of *A Quiet Piece ... for a Violent Time*. Described as "quiet, yes, reassuring, no. Bazelon arrives at his tense purpose through some use of minimalism ... but also through sustained musical line. Jazz elements are introduced in a personal way. Harmonic acidities abound."

141   Gapper, Gordon. "Critics Hear New Music." *The Flint Journal* (November 3, 1963).
Account of the annual meeting of the Music Critics Association in Kansas City. Includes a review of the world premiere of *Symphony No. 1* by the Kansas City Philharmonic. The work is described as being, "to a large extent, an interpretation of New York City", as containing the "imaginative use of opposing and counterpoised sections of the orchestra" and as having "many elevating as well as hectic moments." Also includes a report of Bazelon's contribution to a critics' workshop session, on the relationship between composers, critics and conductors, in which he suggested that the role of the critic should be to narrow "the gulf between composer and conductor a little."

142   Green, Alan. "Bazelon world premiere dazzles." *The Advocate* (May 1, 1985).
Review of the world premiere of *Symphony Concertante*. Described as "a splendid sonic upheaval" and "loud, dissonant and crackling with energy." Also comments that "on one level, it is a study in sonority and orchestral color, rhythm and dynamics analogous to an abstract painting; on another, it expresses our time - full of agitation, nervous tension, complexity and defiance - qualities, according to Bazelon, associated with the city."

143   Green, J. "Modern Composers." *The Harbinger* (Mobile, Alabama) (February 20 - March 4, 1996).
Review of Albany Troy CD174 concentrating on *Symphony No. 7* and *Symphony No. 9 (Sunday Silence)*. Reviews Bazelon's achievement, commenting on his integrity as a composer. Notes that *Symphony No. 9*

"is full of tightly contained potential energy that manages to expend itself without resolving into the expected movement."

144   Griffin, Judson. *Notes: Quarterly Journal of the Music Library Association* (March 1985).
Review of the publication of *Duo for Viola and Piano* by Novello in 1981. Remarks that the title is "apt" in that the work is conceived as a "dialogue" and describes the music as "angular, lively, busy and rhythmic" dealing in "shifting meters and accents in a familiar American style." Also comments on the practical difficulties of the viola part and on the clarity of the manuscript score.

145   Hannigan, Barry. *Notes: Quarterly Journal of the Music Library Association* (September 1991).
Review of the publication of *Re-Percussions* by Novello (Presser) in 1987. The work is compared with *Fiesta* by Lionel Sainsbury. Comments that *Re-Percussions* relies on "short, rhythmic gestures" of a terse character with constant tricky syncopations and shifts of register. Notes the complexity of the formal structure of *Re-Percussions* and that it is "extremely chromatic and dissonant" without being twelve-tone. Summarises the stylistic content, noting that the difficulty of performing the rhythmic patterns accurately would provide "a formidable challenge" for the performers.

146   Haskins, John. "Composer Bets on Horses, Writes Music for Movies." *The Kansas City Times* (November 18, 1970).
Article about the premiere of *Symphony No. Six-Day War* by the Kansas City Philharmonic. It notes that the work was commissioned by Temple B'nai Jehudah as part of their congregation's 100th anniversary commemorations. Some biographical details describe Bazelon "as a Chicago boy, of Spanish and Polish parentage," [in fact his grandparents came from Russia] and his studying composition with Hindemith, Milhaud and Ernest Bloch. Bazelon is described as "a horse player" who was introduced to the sport by Milton Babbitt, explaining: "you know what a mathematical mind Milton has. He figured that with his talents, the track would be a breeze."

147   Haskins, John. "German Pianist Concert Star." *The Kansas City Times* (March 30, 1966).
Review of the world premiere of *Excursion for Orchestra* by the Kansas City Philharmonic. Described as being "remarkably rhythmic in character" with "playful, coloristic touches for orchestra."

148 Haskins, John. "Music in Mid-America." *The Kansas City Times* (November 18, 1970).
Review of the world premiere of *Symphony No. 6*. Notes the origin of the work in a score for a documentary film on Israel's survival in the Six-Day War of 1967. Describes the work as not "descriptive but evocative" and discusses the content of each movement. Includes an account of comments Bazelon made to the audience about the orchestra after the end of the piece.

149 Haskins, John. "Music Makers Discuss Their Art." *The Kansas City Times* (March 5, 1966).
Review of a panel discussion on "The Contemporary Composer" in which Bazelon participated with the conductor Hans Schweiger and the composer Ross Lee Finney, prior to the world premiere of *Excursion for Orchestra* by the Kansas City Philharmonic (in fact postponed because of the illness of key players). Amongst the subjects discussed were the attitudes of conductors to contemporary music and whether composers should write for themselves or for an audience. Bazelon is reported as replying that "he had made up his mind when he became a composer to satisfy himself first." Includes a photograph of the participants.

150 Haskins, John. "Special Jewish Music." *The Kansas City Star* (November 15, 1970).
Article anticipating the world premiere of *Symphony No. Six-Day War*. Includes details of its commission by Temple B'nai Jehudah. Includes a photograph.

151 Hauptman, Fred. *American Music* (Spring 1988).
Review of CRI SD532 which included the *Five Pieces for Piano* and *Imprints*. The *Five Pieces* are described as "fluent." Notes that there is "enough variety and coherence" in *Imprints* "to sustain interest." Also remarks that the impression given by the two pieces is "calmer" than the attributes "nervous, rhythmic, violent" which are more frequently applied to Bazelon's music.

152 Haverstock, Gwendolyn. "An Octogenarian's Music for the Ages." *Newsday* (January 17, 1989).
Review of a concert given to celebrate the eightieth birthday of Elie Siegmeister that included a performance of the *Sonatina for Piano*. Notes that the work has "perpetually moving, motoric outer movements and a still, transparent middle movement."

153 Heise, Kenan. "Irwin Bazelon, Chicago-inspired composer." *Chicago Tribune* (August 5, 1995).

Obituary. Includes an account of his early life in Chicago, his temporary
hearing loss, his studying at DePaul University and his work as a jazz
pianist and a songwriter for a dance band in Chicago. Also describes the
experience of hearing a performance of Beethoven's Seventh Symphony
by the Chicago Symphony Orchestra inspiring him to compose
symphonies and his subsequent composition studies with Hindemith and
Milhaud. Provides a brief review of his achievements as a composer and
notes the fact that "his music was impelled by the big-city sounds he
heard growing up in Chicago." Notes that "acceptance of his classical
pieces was slow in coming" and quotes Bazelon as saying, "when you
stand up there in front of the orchestra and give the downbeat, you forget
all about the frustrations and rejections." Also quotes comments by the
critic David Harold Cox taken from his article in the Bazelon brochure.
Includes a photograph.

154   Henahan, Donal. "Music: Boehm Quintette." *New York Times* (May 24,
       1975).
       Review of the world premiere of the *Woodwind Quintet*. A discussion of
       the style of the work is based on material from the programme notes
       concerning the use of jazz and serial techniques, and their effect,
       apparently indiscernible, upon various aspects of the musical language.

155   Henahan, Donal. "New Bazelon Concerto Led by Pollokoff at 'Y'." *The
       New York Times* (May 18, 1971).
       Review of the world premiere of *Churchill Downs Concerto*. Includes a
       brief account of the scenes during the performance (also described by
       Bazelon in 250) in which "one of America's better-known composers
       [David Diamond] screamed at Mr. Bazelon, who was conducting: 'Go
       study *Le Sacre du Printemps*!' Upon which another member of the New
       York musical community [in fact the artist, Paul Jenkins] leaned over and
       slapped the protester's face." Although the scene brought to mind a
       similar encounter between d'Indy and the aforementioned music of
       Stravinsky in 1914, the piece, however, is described as "an improbable
       one to arouse passions" being "exuberant but musically feeble classicized
       jazz" with a sound and a mood reminiscent of the "more brassily
       pretentious big bands of the nineteen-forties and fifties."

156   Herridge, Frances. "Harlem Group and Gloria Newman." *New York
       Post* (November 7, 1972).
       Review of a performance of *Orbits,* a modern dance choreographed by
       Gloria Newman, to music by Bazelon. Describes the music as
       "atmospheric - dreamy and lingering."

157   Hoffman, Donald. "Composer Exemplifies Rare Breed." *The Kansas City Times* (October 24, 1963).
       Article anticipating the world premiere of *Symphony No. 1* by the Kansas City Philharmonic. Quotes Bazelon as saying "I live in a world of what I call violent silence. I don't hear any outside noise. I block it out and let the inside go" and notes that the "silent world of Irwin Bazelon is a lonely one" and that "the intensity with which he speaks of his craft betrays his loneliness." The composer describes the symphony as a "relentless, impulsive sort of music" using 12-tone techniques without being 12-tone and using jazz effects without being jazz. Also includes Bazelon's comments on the anachronistic position of the composer in the midst of a super-business culture stating that "most people think that for music to have power and dignity and heroic proportions it has to have been written before 1900. Beethoven and Mozart may have had their problems ... but, in a sense, they were mostly financial. I don't think they were faced with anything like the problems we have today - having no performances." Includes a photograph of Bazelon and his wife.

158   Holland, Bernard. "Music: Debuts in Review." *The New York Times* (May 27, 1984).
       Review of the debut recital of William Moersch which included the world premiere of the *Suite for Marimba.* There are no specific comments on the work.

159   Holland, Bernard. "Paying Tribute to Dr. King." *The New York Times* (January 16, 1989).
       Review of a performance of the *Sonatina for Piano* included in a concert designed to celebrate the 80th birthday of Elie Siegmeister. Includes comments on the style of counterpoint in the *Sonatina.*

160   Holly, Rich. "The Modern Marimba." *Percussive Notes* (August 1992).
       Review of CD NDP85528 containing music for marimba played by William Moersch including the *Suite for Marimba.* Comments on the work's "demanding" use of range describing it as "very colorful and exciting." Also notes that the rhythmic usage is original, "with an abundance of polyrhythms and an interesting use of space."

161   Holt, John. "Reader's Choice." *Hi-Fi, Musical America* (May 1973).
       Letter from John Holt referring to the recent issue of CRI SD 287 and describing *Symphony No. 5* as "a fine modern work."

162   Howlett, Christian. "Berkshire Symphony plays eclectic Bazelon piece." *The Williams Record* (April 30, 1985).

Review of the world premiere of *Symphony Concertante for Clarinet, Trumpet and Marimba*. Described as an "unusual and demanding work" whose "overall feeling is disjunct and eclectic." Includes a brief report of a lecture given by Bazelon in which he commented that the piece contains certain "jazz and twelve-tone elements" and notes that the "former are most notable in the solo trumpet and clarinet passages." Includes a photograph of the Berkshire Symphony Orchestra taken during the concert.

163   Hughes, Allen. "Music: Stahl Conducts." *The New York Times* (April 5, 1979).
Review of the world premiere of *De-Tonations*. Largely unfavourable, criticising the continuity of the work in terms of its manipulation of sonority.

164   Hume, Paul. "Bazelon Conducts World Premiere Of His Own Testimonial to a Big City." *The Washington Post* (December 5, 1962).
Review of the world premiere of the *Short Symphony: Testimonial to a Big City*. Comments that "Bazelon finds the energy, the defiant violence, the non-stop restlessness of our large cities an exciting business. He writes in much the same way." Notes that "there is some brilliant scoring" and that "certain touches are of striking beauty and originality, recalling the finest masters of our time." Also includes some, more critical, comments on Bazelon's conducting of the orchestra. This largely favourable review was an important factor in the decision of Boosey and Hawkes to publish the music of Bazelon.

165   Hurd, Michael. *Music in Education* (1977 no. 385).
Review of Bazelon's book *Knowing the Score: Notes on Film Music.* Described as an "elaborate, garrulous and intermittently fascinating book" and although "what he has to say is always pertinent and interesting," it could be said at "half the length." Comments favourably on the generous music examples but is less complimentary about the concluding interviews with film composers, criticising them as "inevitably, scarcely a considered analysis of a complex art."

166   Hutcheson, Thomas. "Trio plays together superbly at MTC's season opener." *The Greenfield Recorder* (July 16, 1996).
Review of a performance of *Alliances* by Dorothy Lawson and Scott Dunn, opening the 27th season of the Mohawk Trail Concerts in Charlemont. Notes that the work spoke "quite clearly and intelligently" giving "the feeling of having travelled to an entirely new place." Discusses the various ways the cello and piano interacted and remarks that although the music was "strange and abrupt" the composer "had

enough in him to speak in a foreign, personal language and still win the audience for his greater alliance."

167   Jenkins, Speight. "David Stahl's Mahler is a National event." *New York Post* (April 4, 1979).
Review of the world premiere of *De-Tonations*. Notes that the composer finds the sound of brass to be suggestive of the "beat of the city," remarking that "the music brought to mind the kind of harsh city sounds most of us try to avoid."

168   Johnson, Bret. *Tempo* (January 1997).
Review of Albany Troy 174 (*Entre Nous, Symphonies Nos. 7 and 9*). Describes *Symphony No. 7* as "an explosively transparent affair, absolutely convincing in its assured touch and instrumentation" and of the last movement in particular remarks that "there seems no limit to the extraordinary sounds he can produce." Comments on the clarity of texture in *Symphony No. 9* and describes it as "masterly."

169   Johnson, Bruce. "Bazelon Premiere Set By Seattle Symphony." *The Tacoma News Tribune and Sunday Ledger* (February 20, 1966).
Article anticipating the world premiere of *Dramatic Movement for Orchestra*. Notes that the composer has already written four symphonies and many other works as well as referring to his music for *The Taming of the Shrew* at the Shakespeare Festival Theater and for the NBC-TV production of *What Makes Sammy Run?*

170   Johnson, Bruce. "Symphony, Cellist Wins Full Applause." *The Tacoma News Tribune* (February 24, 1966).
Review of the world premiere of *Dramatic Movement for Orchestra* by the Seattle Symphony Orchestra. Described as "characterized by a disturbing, almost chaotic theme" but "definitely deserving to be classified with the finest of 20th century symphonic literature." Also quotes Bazelon comments from the programme notes on the inspirational force of his experience of city life, as given in 172.

171   Johnson, Wayne. "Symphony Plays World Premiere." *The Seattle Times* (February 22, 1966).

Review of the world premiere of *Dramatic Movement for Orchestra* by the Seattle Symphony Orchestra. Described as "an intense and excitable work that, according to its composer, contains the 'relentless surge of supercharged city life.' It does indeed reflect the complexities of urban life: the frequent changes of tempo, as well as several tempi existing simultaneously; the involved, new, and frequently cacophonous sounds;

the pushing, pushing, pushing of the complex rhythms and the frequently changing dynamics. It does not embrace and soothe the listener, rather it shocks him with the sounds of modern life which are frequently harsh and disturbing. The principal virtue of the work is its complex, driving rhythmic patterns, especially in the percussion section. These patterns exist not as foundations over which thematic material is constructed, but rather with an assertive and vital independence. Its chief deficiency is one that it shares with many other contemporary compositions: namely an apparent lack of direction and dramatic cohesiveness. The various sections of the work create their own internal character, but this character frequently seems to have little relation to what precedes or follows it. The work creates little sense of dramatic development, of one theme or mood growing out of or into another. But then if the intention of *Dramatic Movement* is to mirror modern urban life, then the work's random, fragmented nature is appropriate." (This review is quoted in its entirety with no changes as a condition of copyright permission being granted for its use.)

172   Johnson, Wayne. "Symphony to Play Bazelon Premiere Tomorrow Evening." *The Seattle Times* (February 20, 1966).
Article anticipating the world premiere of *Dramatic Movement for Orchestra* by the Seattle Symphony Orchestra. Brief biographical details include Bazelon's graduation from DePaul University in 1945, his studying composition with Darius Milhaud for three years and then, during summer sessions, with Ernest Bloch. Notes that his *String Quartet No. 2* was awarded a prize by the National Federation of Music Clubs in 1947, and that in 1957 his *Chamber Symphony for Seven Instruments* was commissioned and performed by the New York Philharmonic Chamber Ensemble conducted by Dmitri Mitropolous. Also describes some of Bazelon's other activities as a professional composer, writing incidental music for the American Shakespeare Festival and the score for the television production of *What Makes Sammy Run?* Includes extensive material taken from the programme notes for *Dramatic Movement* with what is, for Bazelon, an unusually long and explicit description of the formal structure of the work. Also includes a substantial quotation by Bazelon on the underlying aesthetic objective of the work and its origin in the composer's experience of city life: "there is in my music a relentless surge of supercharged city life that reflects the fact that I have lived all my years in the city. The pulse of its rebellious mutterings is omnipresent. The frequent alterations of mood, color, tempo and rhythmic accents in this work are a direct expression of the constant changes of pace inherent in life in a big metropolis, for the city is the grassroots of today. I believe a composer cannot escape his roots and

these origins come to flower in his creative imagination and musical fantasy."

173   Kallai, Sandor.   "Missouri: Operas and Critics." *Musical America* (December 1963).
Review of the world premiere of *Symphony No. 1*. Described as "bold, brassy and brutal" reflecting the composer's experience of city life. Notes a strong jazz influence but remarks that the symphony "is no typical jazz-orientated hybrid work."

174   Kallai, Sandor. "Orchestra Touch to Music of Now." *The Kansas City Star* (October 27, 1963).
Review of the world premiere of *Symphony No. 1* by the Kansas City Philharmonic. Described as being "unquestionably sincere" but "a challenging listening experience" in its "uncompromising brutality." States that the work was introduced by the conductor, Hans Schwieger, who said: "this symphony could not have been written in Paris or Vienna, or in Kansas City or Colorado - only in New York." Even so and despite acknowledging the composer's own comments that the symphony reflects the fact that he has lived his whole life in the city, the reviewer remarks that "surely even in the fiercest urban jungle there is some trace of tenderness, some at least temporary surcease from all this violence" and that even "the softer passages of this work offer virtually no respite," being "as intense as the crashing fortissimos."

175   Kenngott, Louise. "Mime, Sound Join in Winner." *Milwaukee Journal* (March 1, 1979).
Review of a performance of *Sound Dreams*. Describes the musical style of the work and its prevailingly "tranquil" mood, remarking that "only the foghorn of Milwaukee's harbor disturbed the beauty of its performance."

176   Kilpatrick. *American Record Guide* (September/October 1994).
Review of Albany Troy 101. Bazelon is described as a composer with "a distinct voice and something to say." Includes specific comments on *Prelude to Hart Crane's The Bridge, Memories of a Winter Childhood, Symphony No. 8½, Alliances* and *Four... Parts of a World*.

177   Kimball, Robert. "Music Beat." *New York Post* (June 2, 1983).
Review of a concert by the Boehm Quintette which included a performance of the *Woodwind Quintet*. Described as being "full of the sharp punctuations and abrupt mood shifts that characterize city life."

178   Kimmelman, Michael. "Music 55th Anniversary of Composers Group."
       The New York Times (January 13, 1988).
       Review of a concert by the National Association of Composers which
       included a performance of *Fourscore*. Comments favourably upon the
       composer's use of contrasting pace, tension and sonority.

179   Kozinn, Allan. "A Rambunctious Spirit at American Composers
       Orchestra." *The New York Times* (May 14, 1997).
       Review of the world premiere of *Symphony No. 8½* by the American
       Composers Orchestra. Includes comments on the composer's use of
       counterpoint, the character of his melodic lines and the influence of jazz
       on the work.

180   Kozinn, Allan. *ASCAP in Action* (Spring 1981).
       Report on an ASCAP workshop on writing music for films and TV in
       which Bazelon participated. Bazelon describes the advantages of being a
       working professional composer as having an orchestra at your disposal
       and being able to try out new compositional ideas. He also discusses the
       disadvantages remarking that "no composer wants to spend his life
       writing background music. A composer's work is cut, re-cut, and re-
       balanced, sometimes to the point where the composer no longer
       recognises his own score. And because you can always iron out details in
       the studio, film scoring can lead to lazy scoring habits."

181   Kozinn, Allan. "Irwin Bazelon is Dead at 73; Wrote Symphonies and
       Jingles." *The New York Times* (August 4, 1995).
       Obituary. [The headline is partially incorrect, while Bazelon wrote many
       symphonies, he did not write any jingles]. Bazelon is described as a
       composer "whose angular, rhythmically complex and sometimes jazz-
       tinged works evoke the tension, energy and restless drama of
       contemporary urban life." Describes Bazelon's early career, his first
       professional job as a composer and pianist for a dance band in Chicago
       before a concert by the Chicago Symphony Orchestra inspired him to
       write symphonic music. Notes that he studied composition at DePaul
       University, then with Hindemith and Milhaud. Describes his move to
       New York in 1948 where "he worked as a railroad reservations clerk for
       six years before finding a composing job with United Productions of
       America, an animation studio." Discusses his various activities as a
       composer writing music for documentaries and television dramas and
       incidental music for productions of the American Shakespeare Theater.
       His book *Knowing the Score: Notes on Film Music* is described as his
       valedictory farewell to soundtrack composition and a "frank book in
       which he discussed both the artistry and drawbacks of the craft." A
       review of his serious music notes his commitment to symphonic

composition, describing his works as "distinguished ... for their use of elaborate propulsive rhythms" and the eclectic use of "both 12-tone techniques and jazz moves." It is also noted that he "often drew on seemingly conflicting images as in his *A Quiet Piece ... for a Violent Time*" and that he brought "non-musical enthusiasms into his work" capturing his passion for horse-racing in *Sunday Silence* and *Churchill Downs*. Includes a photograph.

182   Kranz, H.B. "An American Symphony." *Aufbau* (December 21, 1962).
       Review of the world premiere of *Symphony No. 2, Testimonial to a Big City*. Bazelon is described as "a master of the modern orchestra, making astoundingly successful use of sonorities which are seldom used by other composers." It notes that the composer has sought to capture the characteristics of an American metropolis, "the rushing tempo of life, in daytime the wildness, defiance, restlessness and confusion, and then at night the ghostly, interrupted silences of an entirely different world."

183   Kranz, H.B. "Grosstadt-Symphonie." *Neue Zeitschrift für Musik* (1963, no. 2).
       Review of the first performance of *Symphony No. 2, Testimonial to a Big City*.

184   Kupcinet, Irv. "Kup's Column." *Chicago Sun Times* (December 20, 1962).
       News item about Bazelon discussing the music for a Nelson Algrea special with Channel 7 officials. Notes that Bazelon is from Chicago and describes the circumstances of his use of Aqueduct winnings of $1000 to record a new composition and playing it to the conductor of the National Symphony, Howard Mitchell, who then invited him to conduct one of his works, ending the account with the remark "saga of a horseplayer!"

185   Kupcinet, Irv. "Kup's Column." *Chicago Sun Times* (December 15, 1977).
       News item about Bazelon writing the music for *Wilma*, an NBC-TV movie being screened later in the week.

186   Lane, Barbara Kaplan. "An Urbanite Composing in Rural Sagaponack." *The New York Times* (January 30, 1994).
       Article anticipating the world premiere of *Entre Nous*. Includes much detailed biographical information, with some material that is not found elsewhere. Describes Bazelon as "an urbanite whose work bristles with the rhythm and hustle of the city" but that he now spends "most of his time in Sagaponack, where he also does much of his composing." Notes that Bazelon has also been inspired by the racetrack and discusses

Churchill Downs. Quotes Bazelon recalling that he "once had an argument with Aaron Copland. He thought that American music was based in the West." Bazelon states that he had "been a city dweller all his life" and that his music could not have been written "by someone who was born and raised in Montana." Bazelon then comments on his relationship with his father describing him as supportive without being able to appreciate his son's music: "he was a bit shocked to discover he had a son who wanted to be an artist but he was always there when I needed him." He also describes his experience of studying composition with Hindemith at Yale: "Hindemith gave me a nervous breakdown, I was much too young to study with him then. He was dogmatic, imperious, intimidating." Bazelon describes his early years as a composer in New York, working for six years as a railroad reservations clerk, before he began to write music for an animation studio, United Productions of America. That led to him writing the music for an Ipana toothpaste commercial which in turn led to his being introduced to documentary film makers like Willard Van Dyke and Ralph Steiner. Other references to his activities at this time include writing music for industrial films about the Air Force and A.T.&T. and for television productions of *What Makes Sammy Run?* and *The Wilma Rudolph Story* as well as comments about his NBC news theme and his book on film music *Knowing the Score.* Of his early career as a composer of music for commercials Bazelon comments: "it gave me a chance to hear my music played by the best musicians in the city." He describes writing music for films as "using 1/17th of your talent." and notes that "film scores are not symphonies, concerti or concert pieces. In the main they consist of short forms ... sketches and fragments of musical seeds - unfinished compositions with only the bare suggestion of character. The end results are abrupt, truncated phrases, mere snatches of music that are all beginning, no middle, and often a welcome end." He also describes a year spent in Hollywood to explore opportunities to write for the movies that caused him to realise that he would never write his symphonies if he stayed there. Bazelon discusses the position of the composer in society and reviews his own achievement as a composer, describing his greatest disappointment as the fact that "the Chicago Symphony, the orchestra that inspired him to make composing his career, has not played any of his music." Notes that he is writing "a symphony based on Hart Crane's *The Bridge.*" Also includes a tribute from the composer to his wife, the artist Cecile Gray Bazelon. Includes a photograph.

187   Larimer, Frances. "New Music Reviews." *Clavier* (January 1997).
       Review of *Sunday Silence* published by Theodore Presser in 1993.
       Includes details of Bazelon's composition teachers and also discusses the
       world premiere of the work.

188   Learmont, John. "Testimonial to a Big City." *National Symphony Orchestra Program* (December 4, 1962).
       Programme note for *Short Symphony, Testimonial to a Big City.* Describes the origins of Bazelon's inspiration in the "frenetic supercharged energy" of the city but states "there is no attempt to be programmatic." Notes certain features of the scoring including the juxtaposition of unusual tone colours, the prominent use of the trumpet, tuba, piccolo and E flat clarinet, and the independent use of percussion all of which contribute to the expression of "the feelings and forward thrust that are inherent in the pulse and rhythm of life today."

189   Lee, Paul. "Discs and Data." *The Witness* (Tallahassee) (April 20, 1972).
       Review of CRI SD287 which includes *Symphony No. 5* and *Churchill Downs.* Includes brief details about the composer and quotes his comments about "the relentless surge of super-charged city life" and "the rhythmic beat of life in the big metropolis." Describes *Symphony No. 5* as "filled with splashes of color" and the end of *Churchill Downs* as "colorful and exciting" and "simply wild."

190   Lehman. "Max Lifchitz Plays American Piano Music." *American Record Guide* (March/April 1992).
       Review of VMM2002 which includes the *Sonatina for Piano.* Described as "concise, rhythmically taut, crisply dissonant" and notes that "the freshness and economy of its neo-classical but atonal two-voice counterpoint are especially pleasing."

191   Lennis, Susan. "Recording in Indianapolis." *The Indianapolis Star Magazine* (January 23, 1972).
       Article on the recording of *Symphony No. 5* by the Indianapolis Symphony Orchestra conducted by Izler Solomon. Includes a long account of the recording process and of the reactions of those involved: the conductor, the composer, the composer's wife, the concertmaster, the producer and the sound engineer. Much of the information provided is of a very detailed nature: the sound engineer, for example, is an "impish-looking man" called David Hancock, who, we are told, has travelled from New York with his equipment in the back of his station wagon, getting lost en route in Columbus, Ohio and then again in Indianapolis itself. A long final section is devoted to Bazelon alone, beginning with his father's intention that his son should be a professional athlete, continuing with his love of horse racing, "the pulse of the track and the rhythm of the city are commensurate - I've gotten some of my best ideas at the racetrack on a Saturday afternoon," his methods of composition which include references to avoiding extensive programme notes because

"whatever intellectual properties are involved are my own and I don't really discuss them" as well as more practical matters such as the need to take time to recharge the creative batteries and a life style that includes "a stringent exercise program three times a week designed to tighten the muscles which become weak when you sit as much as I do." Bazelon also describes his teaching of 45 potential young filmmakers at the School of Visual Arts in New York: "I enjoy teaching these kids because eventually some will make films and when it comes time to choose a composer to write music for their films they will not go down to the local discotheque and hire the bongo player and the electric guitarist but they will know how to communicate with real composers and will expose themselves to music of all kinds." He also offers a range of comments on the profession of being a serious composer within the "greatest super commercial, show business, pop culture ever put on this earth," finishing by remarking that "there's nothing romantic about being a composer. It is the loneliest and most frustrating job in the world. But laying aside all the disappointments and frustrations, when you have a chance to hear your work played by Izler Solomon and the Indianapolis Symphony, you forget all these things." Includes six photographs, the first of the composer, producer and sound engineer in discussion, the second and third of the composer and conductor in conference, the fourth and fifth of adjustments to equipment (it was the orchestra's first recording session for twenty years, hence the interest in the mechanics of the operation) and the sixth of the orchestra in rehearsal.

192   Lensing, Barbara. *"Churchill Downs Concerto* to have its premiere tonight." *The Courier-Journal and Times, Louisville, Kentucky.* (May 16, 1971).
Article announcing the premiere of the *Churchill Downs Concerto* in New York. Comments on the local origins of its inspiration, "when composer Irwin Bazelon went to the Kentucky Derby in 1966 he put his money on Kauai King. The horse won the roses, and Bazelon, carried away with excitement, vowed to capture the whole drama in music." Bazelon states that "the music isn't rock but is in my own language. It's jazzy enough to capture the energy and excitement of the racetrack." Also announces the forthcoming recording of *Symphony No. 5* by the Indianapolis Symphony Orchestra, with the aid of a Ford Foundation grant.

193   Lifchitz, Max. "Sunday Silence: Irwin Bazelon's Final CD Albums." *Composer USA* (Winter 1995-1996).
Obituary and reviews of Albany Troy 054, 101 and 174. Includes biographical details on Bazelon's life, his early composition studies, his activities as a lecturer and writer and on various works with which he and

the author were particularly associated. Describes the origins of Bazelon's musical style in the city and in his personal world of "violent silence" and the nature of his musical language remarking upon its "nervous energy," his use of melody, harmony, rhythm and timbre and the "countless impact-accents" which created "totally unexpected and sudden changes in texture." Discusses the musical content of *Trajectories, Symphony No. 9 (Sunday Silence)* and *Legends and Love Letters* in considerable detail.

194   Livingston, Herbert. *Notes* (June 1957).
Review of the publication of *Five Pieces for Piano* by Weintraub in 1956. Describes the piece as a "set of sensitively-wrought miniatures" including comments about their polyphonic textures, disjunct melodic material, high level of dissonance and "subtle and complicated rhythmic structures." Despite the difficulty of the music for both performer and listener, it is described as "genuinely communicative."

195   Lowens, Irving. "Symphony Concert Spiced by Variety." *Washington Star* (December 5, 1962).
Review of the world premiere of the *Short Symphony, Testimonial to a Big City* by the National Symphony Orchestra. Comments favourably on the orchestration but criticises the work as being "short in musical ideas."

196   Marsh, Robert. "Big city finally hears Bazelon piece." *The Chicago Sun-Times* (December 9, 1984).
Review of the performance of *Short Symphony, Testimonial to a Big City* by the Chicago Civic Orchestra. Notes the work's origin in Bazelon's experience of life in Chicago and remarks upon the length of time (twenty-two years) it had to wait for its local premiere. Describes the middle section as "the most striking and powerful section of the score and the part that best achieves a sense of universality."

197   Mason, Derrick. *Composer* (England) (Summer 1977).
Review of Bazelon's book *Knowing the Score: Notes on Film Music*. Includes a long and thoughtful discussion on the issues raised by the book: the decline of the film music composer's traditional "craftmanship," defined as "adaptability" and a "visual-dramatic talent;" the lack of creative control over the finished product; and the domination of "instant culture cash values." Quotes comments by Leonard Rosenman, Jerry Goldsmith and Elmer Bernstein taken from the interview section of the book. Notes that Bazelon "handles his immense knowledge very skilfully," using incisive, colourful language that the non-musician can always understand. Comments favourably on the content of the opening chapters remarking upon the number of ideas they

contain and the stimulus they provide. Concludes that, although the book is the best he has read on the subject, it is not an "optimistic book" since the film composer needs to be "cunning, compliant, ruthless and, above all, lucky" in order to be successful.

198   McCardell, Charles. "Collage." *The Washington Post* (November 8, 1988).
       Review of the world premiere of *Legends and Love Letters*. Notes that "the setting stood out for the clarity of the vocal line."

199   McGinnis, S. and de Souza, C. "First Performances" *Composer* (London) (Spring 1985).
       Includes factual details, in a list of first performances, of the world premiere of *Fusions*.

200   McMahan, Robert. "*Short Symphony No. 2, Testimonial to a Big City.*" Louisville Orchestra Program Notes (March 15, 1966).
       Programme note for a performance of the *Short Symphony No. 2* by the Louisville Orchestra in 1966. Describes the world premiere of the work as a concert "bristling with the noisy restless tensions and explosive undercurrents of the big city." Discusses Bazelon's writing for documentaries and television films and notes that the composer "makes no distinction between the style or technique used for commercial projects and those destined for the concert hall."

201   McNapsy, C.J. *The Clarion Herald,* New Orleans (November 6, 1975).
       Review of the world premiere of *A Quiet Piece ... for a Violent Time*. Described as "an important new work, well crafted, subtly shaded, evocative of the time we live in."

202   Michaelson, Judith. "New Music to the Ears of the Orchestra League." *Los Angeles Times* (June 23, 1983).
       Article including reference to a performance of *Symphony No. 2* as part of the 38th annual convention of the American Symphony Orchestra League. Reports Bazelon's comments on the increase in the number of contemporary American composers from about 200 in 1948 (when he first came to New York) to about 15,000 and on the infinite variety of the music they write, "some of us dispense amphetamines and some of us dispense soporifics, but there are plenty of us to go around."

203   Milleman, Ginny. "Finding some of the answers behind movie music." *Beaver County Times* (December 27, 1981).
       Review of *Knowing the Score: Note on Film Music*. Discusses the role of music in film examining Bazelon's suggestion that music is "most

effective when it says something not shown on the screen" and explains how music can add "a third dimension to the words and images."

204   Miller, K. "New Music from Leonarda."   *American Record Guide* July/August 1991).
        Review of Leonarda 331 including *Symphony No. 8 for Strings*. Notes that the composer's "technique and sense of timbre are excellent" but that there is "a lack of drama in his music."

205   Monaco, Richard.   *Notes: Quarterly Journal of the Music Library Association* (September 1967).
        Review of the *Brass Quintet* published by Boosey and Hawkes in 1965. Comments on the style of the work describing "the harmonic idiom" as "generally atonal" with "beautifully calculated" sonorities, suggesting that the composer has absorbed elements from "Schoenberg, Webern and jazz." Also discusses the technical demands of the piece, describing the various effects used noting that "the rhythmic demands of the piece are not unreasonable, but a good performance would require many rehearsals."

206   Moore, David. "CRI SD287." *The American Record Guide* (July 1972).
        Review by D.V.M. of CRI SD287 (*Symphony No. 5, Churchill Downs).* Discusses Bazelon's various freelance activities and assesses their effect on his musical expression, noting the way in which "jazz mingles naturally and freshly with his considerable lyricism and with the serious dramatic atmosphere" of a "powerful" Symphony. *Churchill Downs* is described as an "exciting" work with "a most sophisticated use of a brash idiom."

207   Nelson, Boris. "Youth Symphony Delight At Critics' Convention." *The Blade* (Toledo, Ohio) (November 13, 1963).
        Article about the meeting of the Music Critics' Association in Kansas City. Includes a review of a performance of a work by Irwin Bazelon (*Symphony No. 1*) without giving its title. Comments upon the use of "percussion as independent solo instruments" and favouring "brass bombardment and piano declamation against the strings carrying a long singing line." Describes it as "a taxing work, but permeated with ideas and imaginative handling of the orchestral palette."

208   Noble, David. "A Collage of Good Sounds." *The Patriot Ledger,* Boston, Mass. (December 9, 1976).
        Review of the world premiere of *Double Crossings*. Notes that the composer writes TV background music and describes the work as beginning "from materials familiar to police-action adventure fans -

soulful effects from the muted trumpet, sprays of obliquely related percussion events." As the work progressed "it became clear that Bazelon was using this material with an elegance and structural trenchancy that made it true 'classical music'." By the end of the work the reviewer admired Bazelon "for having proven how really musical" his materials "could be when treated so well."

209   Ober, John. *The Patriot Ledger,* Boston, Mass. (January 20, 1981).
       Review of a performance of *Cross-Currents.* Described as "an intriguing and often violent score," and notes the composer's explanation of it as the "embodiment of the rebellious mutterings, cross-rhythms and nervous tension of the city."

210   Page, Tim. "Concert: New York Quintet." *The New York Times* (November 9, 1983).
       Review of a performance of *Quintessentials.* Includes comments about the use of contrasting material for woodwind and percussion.

211   Passey, Charles. "A Classical Role for the Marimba." *Newsday* (March 13, 1988).
       Feature on William Moersch. He describes working with Bazelon to create the *Suite for Marimba.*

212   Patner, Andrew. "Contemporary Chamber Group is in Command of its Music." *The Chicago Sun-Times* (January 26, 1993).
       Review of the Chicago premiere of *Legends and Love Letters.* Described as "beautiful songs with special care taken so that each word and syllable were audible and clear." Comments favourably on the "control and expressiveness" of the singer, Diane Ragain. Notes that the music of the composer "clearly deserves a wider hearing in his home town."

213   Patrick, Corbin. "Cliburn's Eloquence Returns Good Old Days." *Indianapolis Star* (May 9, 1969).
       Review of the world premiere of *Symphony No. 5.* Described as a work that "will give a good deal of pleasure as time goes by." Comments on the use of contrasting tone colours and dynamics, the influence of jazz techniques on the work and the use of dissonance for "accent, variety and dramatic effect without abandoning lyrical charm." Notes that "its style and its pieces meld and the result is attractive." An abridged version appeared in the American Musical Digest (17).

214   Patrick, Corbin. "ISO Goes Modern In Concert." *The Indianapolis Star* (December 3, 1971).

Review of a performance of *Symphony No. 5* by the Indianapolis Symphony Orchestra. Suggests that the work was less successful in the company of an all twentieth-century programme that included Stravinsky's *Pulcinella* and *Symphony of Psalms* than it was in its world premiere two years previously when it was featured with Berlioz and Brahms. Includes specific references to the review of the original performance (213) but remarks that, on this occasion "it did not seem to hang together as well." The critic from The Indianapolis News came to the opposite conclusion (251).

215   Peterson, Melody. "West Coast Premiere." *Los Angeles Times* (October 11, 1971).
Review of a production by the Gloria Newman Dance Theater that included a piece called *Orbits* choreographed by Gloria Newman and danced to recorded music by Irwin Bazelon.

216   Phillips, Karen. "Today's Viola." *The Instrumentalist* (March 1975).
Article on contemporary music for the viola which briefly discusses the *Duo for Viola and Piano*. The writer, who gave the first performance of the work, notes that "the complex rhythms and intricate metric changes require absolute rhythmic precision and complete observation of accents, many of which occur as false downbeats within the bar." Includes a musical example.

217   Pirie, Peter. *The Music Review* (vol. 39, no. 2, 1978).
Review of Bazelon's book *Knowing the Score: Notes on Film Music*. Compares the book unfavourably with *Film Music* (Faber, 1936). Describes the contents as chaotic, mostly concerned "not with technicalities but ham-fisted aesthetics" quoting an example of comments by Leonard Rosenman taken from the section in which he was interviewed. The reviewer is equally dismissive of contemporary film production remarking, somewhat sweepingly, that "few English or American films are worth seeing nowadays."

218   Porter, Andrew. "Musical Events." *The New Yorker* (*June* 4, 1984).
Review of the debut recital of William Moersch which included the world premiere of *Suite for Marimba*. Describes the work as "deftly written" and, in a discussion of the expressive resource of the instrument, notes that Bazelon "deliberately and arrestingly" used "dead strokes" (where the beaters remain in contact with the bars after striking them) "as a shock device" but elsewhere seemed to strive "for bigger sounds" than the marimba could provide.

219   Ralston, Jack. "Symphony No. 6 Day-War." *Kansas City Philharmonic Program Notes* (November 17, 1970).
       Programme note for the world premiere of *Symphony No. 6*. Describes the work's origins in the music written for Jules Dassin's documentary film on Israel, *Survival, 1967*, subsequently developed into a symphony when the composer was commissioned by the Temple Congregation B'nai Jehudah. Quotes Bazelon's comments on the transference from film score to concert hall as being "not a literal one," rather the product of working from "sketches or preliminary drafts." Also quotes Bazelon's comments on his expressive intentions, "I wanted my music to catch a feeling for the Israeli people: their energy, fortitude, drive for survival, will to triumph" without any "deliberate attempt to dramatically describe any aspect of the war in a programmatic form." Includes brief comments on each movement of the work.

220   Rapoport, Paul. "Albany Troy 174." *Fanfare* (May/June 1996).
       Review of Albany Troy 174 (*Entre Nous, Symphonies Nos. 7 and 9*). Describes the music as "utterly idiosyncratic in its disjointed, colorful irregularity." Includes detailed comments on each work.

221   Raush, John. *Notes: Quarterly Journal of the Music Library Association* (March 1996).
       Review of the publication of *Fourscore* by Theodore Presser in 1991. Includes brief biographical details about the composer having studied with Milhaud and Hindemith and states that Bazelon has written symphonies and chamber music including works for percussion ensemble. Describes *Propulsions* as being more adventurous than *Fourscore* whose instrumentation has been scaled down to meet the "practical constraints of a collegiate quartet." Discusses Bazelon's sensitivity to writing for percussion and the rhythmic energy created by "unanticipated accents and rhythmic dislocations," part of an eclectic musical language that is atonal in origin "displaying influences of serial technique, jazz and improvisation." Notes that "the impact of the music is both aural and visual" with a theatrical nature arising from the "often frenetic movements required to perform some of the more rapid passagework."

222   Rice, Pat. "Artists in Profile." *Creative Arts* (Lynchburg, Virginia) (September 27, 1981).
       Article about Bazelon, resident composer at the Virginia Center for the Creative Arts, then at work on *Spires*. Notes the unusual titles and scoring of two recent works: *De-Tonations* and *Partnership* as well as the origin of *Churchill Downs* in Bazelon's love of horse racing and the identity Bazelon finds between city life and the racetrack. Also notes that

Bazelon used his winnings from Aqueduct to record his *Concert Ballet* and that this led to the premiere of his *Short Symphony*. A brief account of his early life includes Bazelon's conversion to serious music on hearing the Chicago Symphony Orchestra when he was 17, a more usual date for this event than that given in 97, his studying music at DePaul University, then "briefly at Yale and with Milhaud on the West Coast" before coming to New York where he worked as a railroad reservations clerk until deciding "I couldn't do it another day or else I'd be a reservations clerk the rest of my life." Also includes a short description of how he rarely composes at the piano, conceiving orchestration and composition simultaneously making little use of an eraser. Reports him as saying, "you really have to want to be a composer to stay in it. When I came to New York, I never knew music was a competitive race. I thought it was a love affair, and I still do." Includes a photograph.

223   Rockwell, John. "Horizons: New-Music Festival Ends." *The New York Times* (June 10, 1984).
      Review of a performance of *Churchill Downs* that ended the New York Philharmonic's Horizons 84 new-music festival. Includes comments on the style of the work that criticise the placing of the work at the end of the programme and the conclusion of the festival.

224   Rockwell, John. "Jonathan Haas Performs Rare Works on Timpani." *The New York Times* (May 25, 1980).
      Review of the New York premiere of *Partnership for Timpani and Marimba*. Comments on the composer's aims and the success with which they were achieved.

225   Rockwell, John. "Tanglewood: Fromm Week Returns to Normal." *The New York Times* (August 4, 1982).
      Review of a performance of *Sound Dreams*. Includes brief comments on the work.

226   Rosell, Juan Pablo. "How a Young Composer Acts at Debut of Opus." *The Seattle Post-Intelligencer* (February 23, 1966).
      Article by "a visiting reporter from Mexico" describing the reactions of Bazelon (and his wife) during the first performance of *Dramatic Movement for Orchestra* and a report of various opinions expressed by composer, conductor and soloist (in the Dvorak Cello Concerto) at the post-concert dinner party. The account is primarily descriptive noting, for example, that during the performance, "from time to time Bazelon jerked his head electrically as if to help the orchestra with the difficult passages."

227   Rosenberg, Donald. "Music famous but not composer Bazelon." *Akron Beacon Journal* (November 6, 1979).
      Article anticipating a performance of *Sound Dreams* and lectures on contemporary music by Bazelon at Akron University. The composer comments on the difficulty of getting his music performed despite the fact that some of it is well known - the seven-second NBC-TV news theme and the 40-second brass and percussion fanfare played at every intermission of Cleveland Orchestra programmes at Blossom Music Center. In the nine years since it was chosen "I haven't been able to get the orchestra to perform more than 40 seconds of my music." Includes significant comments on rhythm, referring to Bazelon's method of composition as often being initially based on rhythmic sketches. Bazelon describes himself as "an old-fashioned composer. Music is an emotional rhythmic experience, not an intellectual exercise. My music has a rhythmic propulsion to it, and people respond to rhythm above anything else. Rhythm is a very primordial part of my body. I suffer a lot from headaches, and that may be because the music I'm writing is diametrically opposed to my heartbeat. Even in relaxation, my music is violent." Bazelon also approves of his wife's definition of his music as "a study in organised hysteria." Includes a photograph.

228   Rosenberg, Donald. "New piano work is impressive." *Akron Beacon Journal* (February 10, 1983).
      Review of the world premiere of *Re-Percussions.* Described as an "impressive work" which "almost belied its title, as the composer avoided the temptation to use the keyboards for bombastic purposes." Notes that "the music did overflow with nervous energy and it captured the ear through a mix of jagged blocks and jazzy rhythmic impulses. The urgency is sustained even in the periods of repose when single sustained tones create mysterious bridges of sound."

229   Rosen, Michael. "Fourscore." *Percussive Notes* (Spring 1987).
      Review of the publication of *Fourscore.* Discusses the composer's use of silence which "further enhances the nature of the restlessness" of the work. Also remarks that "there is an exceptional energy here, punctuated with sforzando attacks, broad strokes of dynamics and an extraordinary use of color." Includes an assessment of the technical difficulties of the work. Uses a number of comments by the composer to illustrate the character of the music.

230   Ross, Alice. "The Horse Who Played Carnegie Hall." *New York Alive,* (May / June 1991).
      Article about *Sunday Silence* and the relationship of the piece to the racehorse. Reprinted in *The Backstretch* (231).

231   Ross, Alice. "Music to My Ears." *The Backstretch* (August 1992).
       Article about *Sunday Silence* and the origin of the piece as a musical
       tribute to the 1989 Horse of the Year. Includes comments on Bazelon's
       love of horse racing and why he was attracted to Sunday Silence in
       particular, "he was dynamic, full of energy, charged with rhythm." Also
       notes that both horse and composer have had to overcome considerable
       obstacles to achieve success. Describes Bazelon's early years in New
       York, working as a railroad reservations clerk arranging passages to
       Florida and writing music in his spare time until he was given the chance
       to write the music for an Ipana toothpaste commercial. Bazelon remarks
       that his commercials "were serious little pieces of music, the same as I
       was writing for the concert hall." Includes references to the NBC News
       Theme and the music for *What Makes Sammy Run?* Other biographical
       details also include an account of Bazelon using his winnings at
       Aqueduct to finance a recording of some of his music which he then used
       to achieve a performance of his *Short Symphony* after which an excellent
       review led to his getting his first publisher. The author concludes with an
       account of the horse's racing career and the decision by Bazelon to make
       an orchestral arrangement of his piano work, creating the only symphony
       ever dedicated to a racehorse. Includes two photographs, one of Bazelon,
       the other of Sunday Silence.

232   Rothstein, Edward. "Music: The Boehm Quintette." *The New York Times*
       (May 30, 1983).
       Review of a performance of the *Woodwind Quintet.* Comments on the
       concert, which included four twentieth-century compositions, as a whole
       and includes a brief reference to Bazelon's use of sound.

233   Sachs, David. "CRI SD486." *Fanfare* (September/October 1983).
       Review of CRI SD486 which included *Sound Dreams.* States that the
       work was written in memory of James Jones and that, without being
       programmatic, it "attempts to express" the composer's feelings about the
       man. Notes that Bazelon's "tribute to his friend is sometimes angry and
       always poignant, dramatic and proudly mournful."

234   Safford, Edwin. "Ensemble to help launch symposium." *The
       Independence Sunday Journal* (March 27, 1985).
       Article anticipating the opening concert of a four-part symposium and
       performance series to be held at Brown University and to include a
       performance of *Sound Dreams.* Includes brief biographical details.

235   Safford, Edwin. "Music was major, technology was minor." *Providence
       Journal-Bulletin* (March 5, 1985).

Review of a performance of *Sound Dreams*. Compares the musical content to the piece's "apparitional title."

236   Salisbury, Wilma. "Fanfare Contest Fulfils Dream." *The Cleveland Plain Dealer* (August 18, 1970).
Article about the Blossom Music Center Fanfare Competition that Bazelon won in 1970 and the composer's enthusiastic reaction to the performance of the fanfare that fulfilled a life's dream to have a piece performed by the Cleveland Orchestra. He is also reported as not believing in composition competitions: "contests are for horses, not people," having only entered two in his life, although he also notes that he won both of them. Bazelon is also quoted as saying: "The world doesn't owe me a living because I write music. I make a living as a composer. But I don't make money at it." Instead he makes money by "playing the horses" and describes his use of his racetrack winnings to record some of his music that led to performances by the National Symphony Orchestra of Washington. Includes a photograph.

237   Schonberg, Harold. "Works of Moderns Heard at Concert." *The New York Times* (March 18, 1950).
Review of the world premiere of *Sonata No. 2 for Piano*. Notes that the composer is being pulled in several directions at once with "neo-classicism, romanticism and a Bartokian rhythmic barbarity all trying to make themselves felt." The composer's struggles to resolve this stylistic disparity are described as "heroic". Also comments upon his sensitivity to melodic pulse and on his "native force and imagination." These remarks are set in the context of a general discussion of the limited musical geometry of modernism as revealed by the works of five young composers in the concert under review. The geometry of Bazelon's music, however, is described as having "a few curves as well as angles and straight lines."

238   Schroeder, Moyra. "Bazelon Dreams of Downs Concerto." *The Louisville Times* (May 11, 1966).
Article about the recording of *Symphony No. 2, Testimony to a Big City* by the Louisville Orchestra. The orchestra and its conductor, Robert Whitney, is praised by Bazelon for their pioneering support of contemporary music. The composer comments, however, that "public acceptance of contemporary music lags far behind" other arts "because most orchestras are museums and their conductors are curators and their audiences think that any piece that was composed since 1900 isn't worth hearing - and here we are almost on the moon!" Other comments on the composer's love of horse racing, his method of picking winners and his recent experience of seeing his first Kentucky Derby anticipating the

composition of the *Churchill Downs Concerto*. There are a number of more personal comments about Bazelon and his wife including the fact that "Bazelon's composing companion is his pet Yorkshire terrier, Clem, named after the famous racehorse." Includes a photograph of the composer, his wife and Robert Whitney.

239   Scott, Kevin. "American Symphonies." *The New York Times* (October 13, 1996).
Letter commenting on the New York Philharmonic's retrospective of American symphonists and their failure to program works by a number of symphonists including Irwin Bazelon.

240   Seabrook, M. "Irwin Bazelon." *Tempo* (April 1996).
Obituary. Notes Bazelon's early life as "a jazz pianist songwriter for Chicago jazz bands," his studies at DePaul, then with Hindemith and Milhaud, his work as a freelance composer in New York and his authorship of *Knowing the Score: Notes on Film Music*. Describes his musical style as "eclectic" but notes also that "his music was accessible and agreeable." Discusses his symphonic output and the fact that "his passionate love of horse racing" led to the composition of *Churchill Downs* and that *Symphony No. 9* is subtitled *Sunday Silence* after a famous American racehorse. Assesses his character as "demonstrative and emphatic" but also "gentle and sensitive" without "an ounce of malice."

241   Sherman, Robert. "5 Composers Hear Brooklyn Ensemble Play Their Works." *New York Times* (April 29, 1975).
Review of the world premiere of *Propulsions*. Includes unfavourable comments on the combined effect of all the works in the programme and criticises the placing of *Propulsions* at the end.

242   Simon, Jeff. "Mini Classic Reviews." *Buffalo Evening News* (December 7, 1974).
Review of CRI 327 (*Propulsions, Brass Quintet*). Describes *Propulsions* as "irresistible" with "great splashes of theatricality." Notes that the composer is "raffish" and "cosmopolitan" with a unique sense of "what will 'play.'"

243   Skei, Allen. *Notes: Quarterly Journal of the Music Library Association* (December 1983).
Review of the publication of the *Woodwind Quintet* by Novello in 1982. Quotes and endorses Bazelon's description (from the sleeve notes to the Orion recording of the work) of the instruments as "protagonists" noting their dual role as both "soloists" and "members of an ensemble."

Discusses Bazelon's imaginative writing for the quintet with the instrumental writing often exploiting the extremes of instrumental ranges with many contrasts "of gesture and phrase," the use of serial pitch organisation and the influence of jazz which creates a "striking rhythmic vitality," noting that "there is nothing static, nothing nebulous about the work; there is instead just a strong sense of direction."

244   Slonimsky, Nicolas. "Irwin Bazelon." *The Concise Edition of Baker's Biographical Dictionary of Musicians,* Schirmer Books, New York (Eighth Edition, 1994).
       Dictionary entry on Bazelon. Includes information on his early musical studies, naming his piano teachers as Irving Harris and Magdalen Massmann, and his composition teachers as Leon Stein, Hindemith, Darius Milhaud and Ernest Bloch. He is incorrectly described as a composer of "commercial jingles." Notes his use of "quaquaversal techniques, ranging from rudimentary triadic progressions to complex dodecaphonic structures" and his preference for "jazz syncopations." Includes a list of works to 1988.

245   Smith, Wayne.   "Angelic Bundle of Art Talents." *The Greenfield Recorder* (January 9, 1974).
       Article on Karen Phillips (viola) quoting Bazelon's description of her as "an angel to see as well as to hear" and noting that she gave the world premiere of his *Duo for Viola and Piano* last summer in Charlemont. Includes a photograph of Karen Phillips.

246   Smith, Wayne. "Premiere By Mohawk Concerts." *The Greenfield Recorder* (August 6, 1973).
       Review of the world premiere of the *Duo for Viola and Piano.* Quotes comments made by the composer about the work including an assertion that it "was not commissioned in the ordinary sense, but completed on returns from a neighboring racetrack." Discusses the work in some detail noting that "there are intervals of great power and themes of exciting beauty." Also comments favourably upon the performance describing that of Karen Phillips in particular as "clear, precise and flawless."

247   Snook, Paul. *Fanfare* (November/December 1992).
       Review of Albany Troy 054 which contains *Spires, Legends and Love Letters* and *Trajectories.* A lengthy, sympathetic and perceptive discussion of Bazelon's musical language, exploring his uncompromising use of dissonance, the city as a major source of his inspiration and the differences in style between his earlier and later music. The reviewer notes that one Bazelonian element less evident in his later music is "the

motoric drive and *allégresse,* the laconic and aphoristic forthrightness ... of his music from the 50s and 60s" as in the *Testament to a Big City (Symphony No. 2)* and *Symphony No. 6.* Even so "the basic and distinctive elements of huge and abrupt dynamic contrasts along with the bristling expressive reserve and withdrawal are still defiantly there." In *Spires* the reviewer finds "the fleeting William Schumanesque vestiges and filtered hints of jazz that are typical of" Bazelon's "less demanding efforts" and in *Legends and Love Letters* he notes "a more lyrically flexible side of Bazelon in an uncharacteristic vocal context." Such a perspective, looking back over a creative evolution of over forty years in length, is unusual in that most commentators on Bazelon's music concentrate on the immediate work.

248   Solomon, Izler. "Orchestras Dead? You're Exaggerating." *The New York Times* (September 14, 1969).
Article including brief reference to the enthusiastic reception given to Bazelon after the world premiere of his *Symphony No. 5* by the Indianapolis Symphony Orchestra as part of an overall discussion of the programming of and positive audience response to an imaginative orchestral repertory.

249   Staff, Charles. "Cliburn Helps Create Rare Musical Beauty." *The Indianapolis News* (May 9, 1969).
Review of the world premiere of *Symphony No. 5* by the Indianapolis Symphony Orchestra. Accounts of the unfavourable response to the work by some in the audience are counterbalanced by comments that "music is a living art" and the "only way to keep it alive" is to "encourage creative artists with performances of their works." Includes a photograph. An abridged version appeared in the American Musical Digest (17).

250   Staff, Charles. "Next Subscription Pair To Include Bazelon's 5th." *The Indianapolis News* (November 26, 1971).
Article anticipating performances of *Symphony No. 5* and its subsequent recording by the Indianapolis Symphony Orchestra for issue by Composers Recording Inc. with *Churchill Downs.* Notes that the symphony is one of a number of works (quoting examples) that were not well received at their first performances. Also includes a description by Bazelon of the first performance of *Churchill Downs:* "a real wild scene developed. I was badly heckled (by a famous American composer, I might add) and with the audience shouting "Bravo" and a general level of wild disorder ... somebody socked the heckler and the security guard was called out, all over a piece of music." Includes a photograph of Bazelon.

251   Staff, Charles. "Symphony and Choir Have Ups And Downs." *The Indianapolis News* (December 3, 1971).
       Review of a performance of *Symphony No. 5* prior to its recording by the Indianapolis Symphony Orchestra for CRI. Notes that the work was given its world premiere by the orchestra two years previously and remarks that "it made a better impression the second time around." Describing the work as "disjunctive music that lacks thrust," but with "a few clear, well-defined ideas" and "splashy and occasionally exciting" orchestral colours, the reviewer comments on the difficulties of understanding the musical argument of such pieces, remarking that although the audience found the work "shocking," it is "actually rather old-fashioned."

252   Starr, Cecile. "Music for Documentaries." *Sightlines* (Summer 1981).
       Review of a panel discussion by composers and film-makers that opened the 1981 American Film Festival. The panel included Virgil Thomson, Amy Rubin, Daniel Schrier, Willard Van Dyke, D. A. Pennebaker and John Duffy. Comments by Bazelon included warnings about the composer's lack of control over the use of his score and about the poor pay of film composers. Even so Bazelon preferred "composing for documentaries to composing for Hollywood" since the "composer's talents are much more appreciated by documentary film-makers." Notes that amongst Bazelon's many film scores is Willard Van Dyke's *Rice* and that he is the author of *Knowing the Score: Notes on Film Music*.

253   Sternfeld, Frederick. *Notes* (March 1955).
       Review of the publication of *Sonatina for Piano* by Weintraub in 1954. Comments that although "the modernity of the music is obvious, its brevity and its leaning in the direction of dodecaphony" is "not contrived." Discusses the middle movement in detail, referring to its "emotional intensity and dignity" and its use of an almost twelve-tone theme that "continues to develop its tragic significance with a noble singleness of purpose right up to the conclusion of the movement."

254   Stromberg, Rolf. "Versatility's the Word." *Seattle Post-Intelligencer* (February 22, 1966).
       Review of the world premiere of *Dramatic Movement for Orchestra* by the Seattle Symphony Orchestra. Described as "an electric work, one of true value" and "energetic and exciting, brimming with high tension." Also notes that Bazelon is a forerunner in a continuing symphonic tradition sustained by the fusion of tradition and a modern idiom.

255   Taylor. "The Modern Marimba." *American Record Guide* (July/August 1992).

Review of CD NDP85528, music for the marimba played by William Moersch, which included the *Suite for Marimba*. The music on the CD is reviewed as a whole and is described as "nothing special" but "well-written" and making "excellent use of the amazing sound of the marimba."

256   Tircuit, Heuwell. "The Modern Marimba." *Fanfare* (May/June 1992).
        Review of CD NDP85528, music for the marimba played by William Moersch, which included the *Suite for Marimba*. Describes the work as "presenting an aggressive stance, highlighted by a driving toccata-like third movement" and comments upon the composer's "effective use" of the lower registers of the instrument.

257   Tircuit, Heuwell. "Modern Classical LPs." *San Francisco Sunday Examiner and Chronicle* (April 23, 1972).
        Review of CRI SD287. Notes that Bazelon's "is a substantive art, one that grows with repeated encounters - modern music of dedication and no gimmicks. He sets out with uncommon purpose towards strength of materials and structure." Of the *Symphony No. 5* the reviewer notes "beautiful music and beautiful writing dominate this piece from the first bar with the most amazing consistency of eloquent statement. This is one of the great American symphonies."

258   Vermeil, Jean. *Repertoire des disques compactes* (March 1993).
        Review of CRI CD623 (*Symphony No. 5, Churchill Downs, Duo for Viola and Piano*). Comments on the use of rhythm and texture, noting the influence of jazz.

259   von Rhein, John. *Chicago Tribune* (December 10, 1984).
        Review of a performance of *Short Symphony, Testimonial to a Big City* by the Civic Orchestra of Chicago. The work is described as being "a seriously intended work of sinew and substance that has something to say and says it with directness and vigour" and "characterised by aggressive rhythms that surge across bar lines with a uniquely American energy." Remarks of "the frenetic bursts of activity and tense silences" that "one doesn't have to know that Bazelon worked for a time with Dave Brubeck to appreciate his deft deployment of jazz rhythms." [In fact Brubeck and Bazelon were just pupils of Milhaud at the same time; there is no evidence that they worked together]. Also notes that, although the composer is a native of Evanston and a graduate of DePaul University, and that his output is large and has been performed by leading musicians of America and Europe, "the sad fact is that the Chicago Symphony Orchestra has never played a note of his music."

260   Vourhees, John. *The Seattle Post-Intelligencer* (March 22, 1966).
       Review of a King-TV documentary on the Seattle Symphony Orchestra
       including the preparation for and the premiere of *Dramatic Movement for
       Orchestra.* Described as a work "which seemed attractive but of no great
       depth or profundity. It was fashionable music with plenty of percussion,
       admirably controlled, but often sounding like the kind of soundtrack
       music that signifies 'the urban scene.'"

261   West, Dick. "Gambling Genius Parlay Pays Off." *News Register*
       (Wheeling, West Virginia) (December 3, 1962).
       Article same as 262.

262   West, Dick. "Incredible Story of Irwin Bazelon." *Sarasota News*
       (December 4, 1962).
       Article about Bazelon and the forthcoming world premiere of his *Short
       Symphony, Testimonial to a Big City.* Includes a description of the events
       leading to the work being accepted for performance by the National
       Symphony Orchestra.

263   Wheeler, Scott. *Fanfare* (November/December 1992).
       Review of CRI American Masters Series CD623, including *Symphony
       No. 5, Churchill Downs Chamber Concerto, Duo for Viola and Piano*
       and *Propulsions.* Bazelon is described as "one of the most underrated of
       American Masters." His music is described as never seeming "to wander
       in search of images, unlike that of some other successful film
       composers." It "retains a sense of continuity and structure that is well
       grounded in the music itself." *Symphony No. 5* is described as a
       "compelling orchestral work" with moments of "intense, austere beauty"
       and throughout "a dark sense of New York City, reminiscent of *film noir,*
       and beneath the free use of serial techniques runs an undercurrent of
       jazz." This "subtle jazz flavour becomes explicit in the *Churchill Downs
       Chamber Concerto"* which is a work that "has a brightness that reflects
       the manic side of city life."

264   Whitaker, William. "Score Analyzes Film Music." *The Abilene
       Reporter* (February 1982).
       Review of *Knowing the Score: Notes on Film Music.* Described as an
       "analytical, policy document on the subject." Explores various issues
       including the degree of artistic freedom that a film composer has and the
       conservative nature of much film music composition. Discusses
       Bazelon's comments on Max Steiner in some detail. Also comments on
       Bazelon's exploration of the "psychological implications of music in
       films" supported by a wide range of examples. Describes the final section
       of interviews as "absorbing."

265   White, Jean. "Highly Touted Composer Nears the Home Stretch." *The Washington Post* (December 2, 1962).
        Article anticipating the world premiere of the *Short Symphony, Testimonial to a Big City* by the National Symphony Orchestra. Based on an extensive interview with the composer, it includes comments on his love of horse racing, "the pace of the race track catches all the pulse of the city and its inhabitants - hope, anxiety, joy, disappointment, all capsuled in a one-minute race," on the need to support the work of serious composers, "there should be some kind of Federal bank where artists can go and get a long-term, low-interest loan" and on music education "I would do away with all music appreciation courses." On the symphony the composer stated, "the city is the grassroots of today. I'm tired of composers from Brooklyn who write about mountains and plains and the Golden West. The city is frenetic, hard-driving; there is nothing particularly delicate about it." Includes a photograph.

266   Zakariasen, Bill. "A musical success from an unusual marriage." *Daily News* (New York) (June 12, 1984).
        Review of a performance of *Churchill Downs*. Comments that "despite its dated qualities, it proved enjoyable."

267   Zakariasen, Bill. "Good new stick man." *Daily News* (April 5, 1979).
        Review of the world premiere of *De-Tonations*. Described as "monstrously overlong for its non-existent quality of material."

268   Ziegler, Roger. "Last Interview: Composer for 21st Century." *The Southampton Press* (August 17, 1995).
        Article about an interview given by Bazelon one week before his death. The composer discusses the lack of recognition of his music, proposing the establishment of a "Society for the Preservation of Unpopular Music" to counteract "the pop songwriters and rockers" who "get all the attention in our society." The author notes that "Bazelon's music was an unfiltered extension of the man himself, totally uncompromising, completely original and utterly without pretence and artifice." He also comments on the strange decision of one local radio station to broadcast a work by Benjamin Britten in Bazelon's memory rather than choosing one of the composer's own orchestral works. The theme of neglect also underlies many of Bazelon's comments. "You have to realise we are living in the greatest super-business society ever put on this earth. A society which has spawned an elephantine pop music culture inculcating millions of impressionable adolescents with the incredible idea that showbiz, song hits, celebrityhood and culture are synonymous terms. They are not synonymous terms." and "People say to me, 'why don't you write something pleasant and flowing?' and I always reply, 'we're five years

away from the year 2000, what do you want, more Brahms?' " Includes a brief account of Bazelon's creative life, his playing jazz piano in local jazz clubs in Chicago before "a life-transforming event" of hearing the music of Beethoven, graduating from DePaul University, and studying composition with Hindemith and Milhaud. There are also more personal comments by the composer including one about his mother's lack of understanding of his desire to be a composer: "she never understood this is what I had to do" and "when I was 46 she said to me, 'you know, it's not too late to go to law school.'" [In fact this advice, which Bazelon often recalled, would have been given much earlier in his life, probably in the early 1950s, before he started to make a living from composition.] Describes Bazelon's career as a professional composer writing music for animation shorts, documentary films and television, including the NBC news theme and *What Makes Sammy Run?*, experiences distilled in his book *Knowing the Score: Notes on Film Music.* Among comments on his serious composition are references to a recent performance of *Fire and Smoke* at the Aspen Music Festival in 1994, a projected performance of *Spires* in Chicago conducted by Boulez, and the recent recording of the seventh and ninth symphonies by the Bournemouth Symphony Orchestra. In a final comment anticipating his own mortality, Bazelon remarks, "I'm not afraid of death; the only thing that scares me is St. Peter and the angels greeting me at the gate with electric guitars instead of harps." Includes a photograph.

Discography

Alliances
    Albany Records Troy 101 / 1993 / CD
    Dorothy Lawson, cello; Michael Boriskin, piano.
    Includes: *Dramatic Fanfare, Memories of a Winter Childhood, Symphony No. 8½, Prelude to Hart Crane's "The Bridge," Four ... Parts of a World.*

A Quiet Piece . . . for a Violent Time
    Albany Records Troy 370 / 1999 / CD
    Rousse Philharmonic conducted by Harold Farberman.
    Includes: *Symphony No. 4, For Tuba . . . with Strings Attached*

Brass Quintet
    CRI SD327 / 1974 / LP
    American Brass Quintet.
    Includes: *Propulsions.*

Churchill Downs
    CRI SD287 / 1972 / LP and Cassette
    Chamber Ensemble conducted by the composer.
    Includes: *Symphony No. 5.*

    CRI American Masters Series CD623 / 1992 / CD
    Chamber Ensemble conducted by the composer.
    Includes: *Propulsions, Symphony No. 5, Duo for Viola and Piano.*

Cross-Currents
Albany Records Troy 282 / 1998 / CD
Jonathan Haas, percussion; Neil Balm, Raymond Mase, trumpets; Jeffrey Lang, French horn; James Pugh, trombone; Marcus Roja, tuba.
Includes: *Fairy Tale, Re-Percussions, Vignette, Fusions.*

Dramatic Fanfare
Albany Records Troy 101 / 1993 / CD
Vancouver Symphony Orchestra conducted by Harold Farberman.
Includes: *Memories of a Winter Childhood, Symphony No. 8½, Prelude to Hart Crane's "The Bridge," Alliances, Four ... Parts of a World.*

Duo for Viola and Piano
CRI 342 / 1975 / LP
Karen Phillips, viola; Glenn Jacobson, piano.
Includes: Paul Lansky, *Modal Fantasy*; Raoul Pleskow, *Motet and Madrigal,* Mark Zuckerman, *Paraphrases*; Lowell Cross, *Three Etudes for Magnetic Tape.*

CRI American Masters Series 623 / 1992 / CD
Karen Phillips, viola; Glenn Jacobson, piano.
Includes: *Symphony No. 5, Churchill Downs, Propulsions.*

Entre Nous
Albany Records Troy 174 / 1995 / CD
Dorothy Lawson, cello; Bournemouth Symphony Orchestra conducted by Harold Farberman.
Includes: *Symphony No. 7, Symphony No. 9.*

Fairy Tale
Albany Records Troy 282 / 1998 / CD
Lois Martin, viola; Chamber Ensemble conducted by Harold Farberman.
Includes: *Re-Percussions, Cross-Currents, Vignette, Fusions.*

Five Pieces for Piano
CRI SD532 / 1986 / LP and Cassette
Wanda Maximilien, piano.
Includes: *Imprints ... on Ivory and Strings,* Ellie Siegmeister, *Ways of Love, Five Langston Hughes Songs.*

For Tuba ... with Strings Attached
Albany Records Troy 370 / 1999 / CD
Rousse Philharmonic conducted by Harold Farberman.
Includes: *Symphony No. 4, A Quiet Piece ... for a Violent Time.*

Four . . . Parts of a World
>   Albany Records Troy 101 / 1993 / CD
>   Joan Heller, soprano; Thomas Stumpf, piano.
>   Includes: *Dramatic Fanfare, Memories of a Winter Childhood, Symphony No. 8½, Prelude to Hart Crane's "The Bridge," Alliances.*

Fourscore
>   New World Records 382-2 / 1989 / CD
>   Continuum Percussion Quartet.
>   Includes: John Cage, *Third Construction*; Eugene Kurtz, *Logo 1*; John Ver-Planck, *Petite Suite*; Christopher Rouse, *Ku-Ka-limoku*; Lou Harrison, *Violin Concerto.*

Fusions
>   Albany Records Troy 282 / 1998 / CD
>   Paul Lustig Dunkel, flute/piccolo; Randall Wolfgang, oboe/English horn; Mitchell Estrin, clarinet; Dennis Smylie, bass clarinet; Marc Goldberg, bassoon/contrabassoon; Jeffrey Lang, French horn; Neil Balm, Raymond Mase, trumpets; James Pugh, trombone; Jonathan Haas, percussion; John Van Buskirk, piano; Lois Martin, viola; Jeff Carney, bass; conducted by Harold Farberman.
>   Includes: *Fairy Tale, Re-Percussions, Cross-Currents, Vignette.*

Imprints . . . on Ivory and Strings
>   CRI SD532 / 1986 / LP
>   CRI Cas532 / 1986 / Cassette
>   Wanda Maximilien, piano.
>   Includes: *Five Pieces for Piano,* Elie Siegmeister, *Ways of Love, Five Langston Hughes Songs.*

Legends and Love Letters
>   Albany Records Troy 054 / 1992 / CD
>   Joan Heller, soprano; Collage New Music Ensemble conducted by Charles Fussell.
>   Includes: *Spires, Trajectories.*

Memories of a Winter Childhood
>   Albany Records Troy 101 / 1993 / CD
>   Vancouver Symphony Orchestra conducted by Harold Farberman.
>   Includes: *Dramatic Fanfare, Symphony No. 8½, Prelude to Hart Crane's "The Bridge," Alliances, Four ... Parts of a World.*

Midnight Music
>   Doyen Wind Band Series Doy 037 / 1994 / CD

Royal Northern College Wind Orchestra conducted by Timothy Reynish. Includes: Richard Rodney Bennett, *Four Seasons, Morning Music, Trumpet Concerto.*

Overture to Shakespeare's "The Taming of the Shrew"

Albany Records Troy 380 / 1999 / CD
Rousse Philharmonic conducted by Harold Farberman.
Includes: *Symphony No. 2 (Short Symphony), Symphony No. 6.*

Prelude to Hart Crane's "The Bridge"

Albany Records Troy 101 / 1993 / CD
Chicago String Ensemble conducted by Alan Heatherington.
Includes: *Dramatic Fanfare, Memories of a Winter Childhood, Symphony No. 8½, Alliances, Four ... Parts of a World.*

Propulsions

CRI SD327 / 1974 / LP
Percussion Ensemble conducted by the composer.
Includes: *Brass Quintet*

CRI American Masters Series 623 / 1992 / CD
Percussion Ensemble conducted by the composer.
Includes: *Churchill Downs, Symphony No. 5, Duo for Viola and Piano.*

Re-Percussions

Albany Records Troy 282 / 1998 / CD
Richard Rodney Bennett and Scott Dunn, pianos.
Includes: *Fairy Tale, Cross-Currents, Vignette, Fusions.*

Short Symphony, Testament to a Big City

First Edition Records L-664 / 1967, 1975, 1980 / LP
(Same performance, issued with different record covers)
Louisville Orchestra conducted by Robert Whitney.
Includes: Gian Francesco Malipiero, *Notturno di Canti e Balli.*

Albany Records Troy 380 / 1999 / CD
Rousse Philharmonic conducted by Harold Farberman.
Includes: *Overture to Shakespeare's "The Taming of the Shrew," Symphony No. 6.*

Sonatina for Piano

Vienna Modern Masters VMM2002 / 1991 / CD
Max Lifchitz, piano.

Includes: Emma Diemer, *Encore*; Sherwood Shaffer, *Lines from Shelley*; Elizabeth Bell, *Night Music*; Laura Greenberg, *Cycles*; de la Vega, *Homenagem*; Steven Strunk, *Prisms*; Howard Quilling, *Piano Sonata No. 3*.

Sound Dreams
CRI SD486 / 1983 / LP
Collage New Music Ensemble conducted by Gunther Schuller.
Includes: Leonard Rosenman, *Chamber Music V*; John Hess, *Capriccio*.

Spires
Albany Records Troy 054 / 1992 / CD
Maurice Murphy, trumpet; London Philharmonic Orchestra conducted by Harold Farberman.
Includes: *Trajectories, Legends and Love Letters*.

Suite for Marimba
Newport Classic Premier NPD85528 / 1992 / CD
William Moersch, marimba.
Includes: Jacob Druckman, *Reflections on the Nature of Water;* Andrew Thomas, *Merlin*; Martin Wesley-Smith, *For Marimba and Tape*; Richard Rodney Bennett, *After Syrinx II*.

Symphony No. 4
Albany Records Troy 370 / 1999 / CD
Rousse Philharmonic conducted by Harold Farberman.
Includes: *A Quiet Piece . . . for a Violent Time, For Tuba . . . with Strings Attached*.

Symphony No. 5
CRI SD287 / 1972 / LP and Cassette
Indianapolis Symphony Orchestra conducted by Izler Solomon.
Includes: *Churchill Downs*.

CRI American Masters Series 623 / 1992 / CD
Indianapolis Symphony Orchestra conducted by Izler Solomon.
Includes: *Churchill Downs, Propulsions, Duo for Viola and Piano*.

Symphony No. 6
Albany Records Troy 380 / 1999 / CD
Rousse Philharmonic conducted by Harold Farberman.
Includes: *Overture to Shakespeare's "The Taming of the Shrew," Symphony No. 2 (Short Symphony)*.

Symphony No. 7 (Ballet for Orchestra)
Albany Records Troy 174 / 1995 / CD
Bournemouth Symphony Orchestra conducted by Harold Farberman.
Includes: *Entre Nous, Symphony No. 9.*

Symphony No. 8 for Strings
Leonarda Records CD LE 331 / 1990 / CD
London Philharmonic Orchestra conducted by Harold Farberman.
Includes: Donald Erb, *Contrabassoon Concerto*; Marga Richter, *Blackberry Vines*; Erik Lundborg, *Switchback.*

Symphony No. 8½
Albany Records Troy 101 / 1993 / CD
Vancouver Symphony Orchestra conducted by Harold Farberman.
Includes: *Dramatic Fanfare, Memories of a Winter Childhood, Prelude to Hart Crane's "The Bridge," Alliances, Four ... Parts of a World..*

Symphony No. 9 (Sunday Silence)
Albany Records Troy 174 / 1995 / CD
Scott Dunn, piano; Bournemouth Symphony Orchestra conducted by Harold Farberman.
Includes: *Entre Nous, Symphony No. 7.*

Trajectories
Albany Records Troy 054 / 1992 / CD
Wanda Maximilien, piano; London Philharmonic Orchestra conducted by Harold Farberman.
Includes: *Spires, Legends and Love Letters.*

Vignette
Albany Records Troy 282 / 1998 / CD
John Van Buskirk, harpsichord.
Includes: *Fairy Tale, Re-Percussions, Cross-Currents, Fusions.*

Woodwind Quintet
Orion Master Recordings ORS78291 / 1977 / LP
Boehm Woodwind Quintette.
Includes: Franz Danzi, *Bläserquintett in G, Op. 67, No.1*; J. Guy Ropartz, *Deux Pièces.*

Library Music recorded under the pseudonym of Budd Graham.

Clem's Capers	(6)
Country Hay-Ride	(4)
Dance for a Tomboy	(2)
Dance for 2 Chickens and 7 Eggs	(7)
Little Miss-Summer-Night Dream	(7)
Lyric Piece	(2)
Parade of the Taxicabs	(6)
Pastoral	(1)
Propellers and Open Cockpits	(4)
Restless Colors in a Quiet Frame	(8)
Slow March for a Robot	(6)
The Animated Scarecrow	(7)
Volcanic Events	(5)
Walking Through the City	(3)
3½ Men on a Horse	(7)

(1) Boosey and Hawkes SBH 3004 / 1968 / LP   New Concert Orchestra
(2) Boosey and Hawkes SBH 3011 / 1969 / LP   New Concert Orchestra
(3) Boosey and Hawkes SBH 3012 / 1969 / LP   New Concert Orchestra
(4) Boosey and Hawkes SBH 3020 / 1970 / LP   New Concert Orchestra
(5) Boosey and Hawkes SBH 3029 / 1971 / LP   New Concert Orchestra
(6) Boosey and Hawkes SBH 2992 / 1972 / LP   New Concert Orchestra
(7) Boosey and Hawkes SBH 3037 / 1972 / LP   New Concert Orchestra
(8) Boosey and Hawkes SBH 3055 / 1974 / LP   Sound Studio Orchestra

Archive Collections

(1) Irwin Bazelon Collection. Library of Congress, Washington D.C. Established 1997.

The archive is divided into two sections and is arranged in 35 boxes.

Bazelon's music is housed in boxes 1-32 as follows:

Boxes 1-15: Original manuscripts in the composer's hand. Each one is given in the chronological list of works. A number of original manuscripts have been lost.

Boxes 16-19: Photocopies of works no longer existing in the original manuscript. These boxes also contain copies of some early works reproduced from transparencies.

Boxes 20-30: Copies of film, broadcast and library music arranged as follows:

Boxes 20-21: Documentaries.

Boxes 22-23: Industrials.

Boxes 24-25: Commercials.

Boxes 26-28: TV shows and movies.

Box 29: Incidental music.

Box 30: Library music for Boosey and Hawkes.

Box 30 also includes miscellaneous sketches (including a *String Quartet*).

Boxes 31-32: Copies of printed music. Many of these works were published by reproducing the composer's manuscript.

Bazelon's personal papers are housed in boxes 33-35 as follows:

Box 33:   Biographical materials.
               Correspondence.
               Business papers.
This section includes publishing contracts with Peer International
Corporation (1950), Weintraub Music Company (1953-1956), Boosey
and Hawkes (1963-1970), Novello (1978-1990), and the Theodore
Presser Company (1990-1995).
Box 34:   Programmes.
               Programme notes.
Box 35:   Reviews.
               Flyers.
               Research materials for Bazelon lectures.
               Bazelon's writings.
               Miscellaneous documents.

The collection also includes a group of works described as juvenilia. This
designation is at least partially inaccurate since the group includes some
significant works composed during his twenties. At some point in his life,
however, Bazelon separated them from his other works by putting them into
storage where they remained until after his death. These works have not yet
been allocated a box number in the Bazelon Collection in the Library of
Congress. They are described in this book as being located in box J, a
designation adopted to prevent confusion between the original numbering of the
collection and a recent rearrangement of the material. It is possible that this
group of works only represent a fraction of the music that Bazelon composed in
his youth and that many other pieces have not survived.

A number of commercial works only survive as recordings. These works have
also not yet been allocated a box number in the Bazelon Collection and are
described in this book as being located in box R.

(2) The Leon Stein Collection. The John P. Richardson Library, DePaul
University, Chicago.

The collection contains a considerable number of letters written by Bazelon to
his first composition teacher Leon Stein. The correspondence begins with a
letter written in 1946 while Bazelon was studying with Milhaud in California
and another written in 1947 from New York when Bazelon was attempting to
settle there. The correspondence resumes in 1965 and continues until 1987. It
includes comments about Bazelon's creative intentions, plans for future
performances, and frankly expressed views on a number of significant issues.

(3) The Irwin Bazelon Collection. Harold B. Lee Library, Brigham Young
University, Provo, Utah.

The collection contains correspondence concerning the publication of *Knowing the Score: Notes on Film Music* and six audio cassettes of interviews with film composers featured in the book: Elmer Bernstein, Paul Glass, Jerry Goldsmith, Gail Kubik, Johnny Mandel, Alex North, David Raskin, Leonard Rosenman, Laurence Rosenthal, Bernardo Segull, Lalo Shriffrin, and John Williams.

Index of Bibliographical References

(b) References to other works

Commercials
7, 42, 97, 98, 99, 128, 133, 181, 186, 230, 231, 244

Buitoni	7, 133
Ipana	7, 133, 186, 230, 231
Noxzema	7, 133
Peerless Pickle Company	128

  Note: The Peerless Pickle Company reference was to an imaginary
  product.

Documentaries, Films and Television
  6, 7, 24, 32, 37, 39, 42, 43, 44, 47, 89, 95, 99, 111, 126, 128, 133,
  139, 153, 169, 172, 180, 181, 184, 185, 186, 219, 230, 231, 252, 260,
  265, 268

Air Force	186
Armstrong Circle Theatre Opening	128
A.T.&T.	186
The Hope that Jack Built	37
The Human Element	39
The Ivory Knife	47
Rice	252
Standard Oil	128
Survival 1967	24, 89, 133, 139, 148, 219
U.S. Steel	265
What Makes Sammy Run?	24, 43, 111, 133, 169, 172, 186, 230, 231, 268
Wilma	43, 111, 133, 185, 186

Incidental Music
  30, 32, 42, 43, 111, 112, 121, 128, 133, 139, 156, 169, 172, 181, 215,
  265

American Shakespeare Festival Theater	32, 42, 43, 111, 121, 128, 133, 139, 169, 172, 181, 265
Frankie and Johnny	30
Orbits	112, 156, 215

NBC-TV News Theme
  7, 42, 73, 128, 133, 139, 153, 181, 186, 227, 230, 231, 236, 268

(c) Reviews of Recordings

(d) Reviews of Knowing the Score: Notes on Film Music

Other references to *Knowing the Score: Notes on Film Music*.

(e) Chronological Index of Bibliographical References

Index

Note: Authors cited in the Bibliography are only included in this index if they are mentioned in other references. For references to Bazelon's works, consult the alphabetical list of works in the Index of Bibliographical References.

About the Author

DAVID HAROLD COX is Professor of Music at University College Cork in the Republic of Ireland. He is a composer, musicologist and performer.

ISBN 0-313-30550-1

90000>

E AN

9 780313 305504

HARDCOVER BAR CODE